Visual QuickStart Guide

DOS 6

Christopher Nye
Suzie Wynn Jones
David Webster

Webster & Associates

Peachpit Press

DOS 6: Visual Quickstart Guide
Webster & Associates

Peachpit Press, Inc.
2414 Sixth Street
Berkeley, CA 94710
(510) 548-4393
(510) 548-5991 (fax)

Notice of Liability

Trademarks

ISBN: 1-56609-059-8
Printed and bound in the United States of America

 Printed on recycled paper

Why a Visual QuickStart?

Virtually no one actually reads computer books—instead, people use them as references. This series of **Visual QuickStart Guides** has made that reference easier thanks to a new approach to learning computer applications.

Conventional computer books usually teach you about a program using extensive textual explanations. A **Visual QuickStart Guide** takes a far more visual approach—pictures literally show you what to do, and text is limited to clear, concise commentary. Learning is easier, because a **Visual QuickStart Guide** familiarizes you with the look and feel of your software. Learning also becomes faster, because you don't have to comb through long-winded passages to find the information you need.

It's a new approach to computer learning, but it's also solidly based on experience: Webster & Associates have logged thousands of hours of classroom computer training, and have authored many books on computer applications.

Chapter 1 introduces you to basic MS-DOS concepts.

Chapter 2 introduces you to basic PC concepts.

Chapters 3 through **10** outline graphically the major MS-DOS and PC features. These chapters are easy to reference and use screen shots to ensure that you grasp concepts quickly.

Acknowledgments

The authors wish to acknowledge the effort and dedication of the following people:

- Stephanie Berglin
- Jenny Hamilton
- Sean Kelly, Editor
- Paul McCarthy
- Mark Sefein
- Tony Webster

Contents

Chapter 4: Command Line Survival (cont.)

Chapter 5: MS-DOS Shell

Chapter 6: MS-DOS Editor

Chapter 7: In Charge of your System

Chapter 8: Advanced Command Techniques

Chapter 9: Customizing Your PC

Chapter 10: Windows Programs

Index

WHAT IS MS-DOS?

DEFINITION

All computers need an operating system. An operating system is a set of instructions that controls your personal computer (PC). Most PCs today use MS-DOS.

Your computer accesses MS-DOS instructions as soon as you start it. MS-DOS then runs in the background, organizing all the tasks your computer performs.

Figure 1. MS-DOS stands for "Microsoft Disk Operating System." "Microsoft" is the name of the company that developed MS-DOS. "Disk Operating System" indicates the function of MS-DOS, which is to operate the computer. More simply, it makes the computer work!

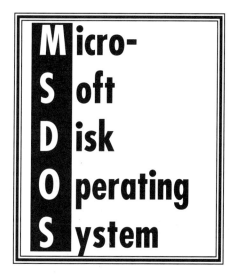

OPERATING SYSTEM

Think of MS-DOS as the president of a company. The role of a president is to coordinate the company so that it runs efficiently. The role of MS-DOS is to coordinate all the functions of a computer so that it, too, runs smoothly.

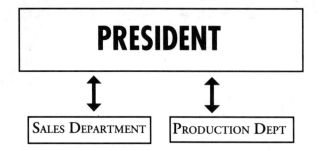

Figure 2. The president relies on management and staff to perform certain tasks; in a manufacturing company, for example, the production department builds the products and the sales department sells them.

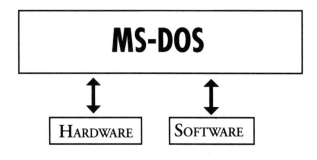

Figure 3. MS-DOS manages "hardware" and "software" in much the same way.

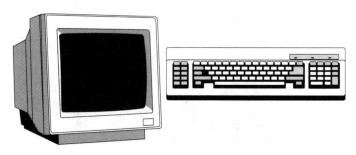

Figure 4. "Hardware" is computer equipment such as a keyboard or screen. A keyboard collects information from the user and the screen displays it.

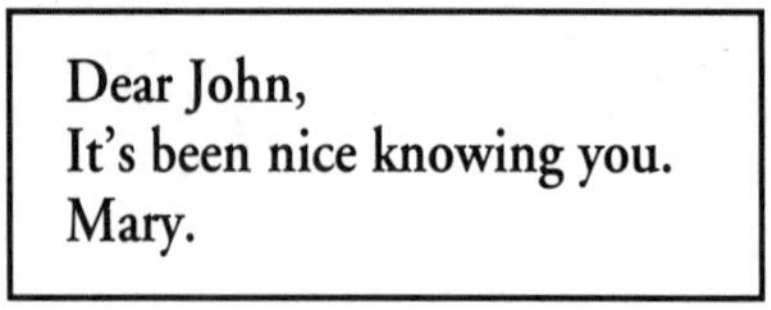

Dear John,
It's been nice knowing you.
Mary.

Figure 5. "Software" is a set of instructions that tells your PC how to perform a specific task.

For example, a word processing program is software you can use to write a letter.

Figure 6. The computer stores this information in a "file." A file could be a letter you wrote using a word processing program. MS-DOS enables you to issue commands that manage your files.

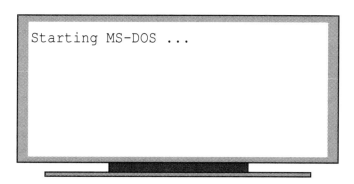

```
copy letter.doc a:
```

Figure 7. MS-DOS determines what happens when you start your computer. This is called a "start-up procedure." Computer manufacturers usually install MS-DOS and set the startup procedure before you buy the computer. You can change the startup procedure using MS-DOS.

```
Starting MS-DOS ...
```

VERSIONS

MS-DOS has been available since 1981. The first version was 1.0. Since then, Microsoft has updated it several times. The current version is 6.0, which this book covers.

PC Fundamentals

Computer Components

This chapter covers the standard pieces of equipment—known as hardware—that your computer needs to manipulate data.

Figure 1. A PC follows a three-stage process: inputting data, processing it, and outputting the result. You can add a fourth stage to the process by storing the data permanently. The flow chart below illustrates this process.

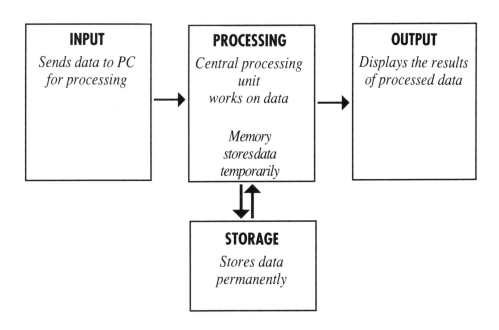

INPUT	**PROCESSING**	**OUTPUT**
Sends data to PC for processing	*Central processing unit works on data* *Memory stores data temporarily*	*Displays the results of processed data*

STORAGE

Stores data permanently

INPUT

Inputting data is your first step in using a PC. You input data with an input device. There is a wide range of input devices available; the most common are keyboards and mice.

KEYBOARDS

Figure 2. There are many styles of keyboards. The two most common are the XT and AT (enhanced) keyboards. The AT has extra keys, including a cursor movement keypad and the F11 and F12 function keys.

The AT keyboard

The XT keyboard

MOUSE

Figure 3. The mouse is an input device that can select and move objects around the screen. The mouse on your desk controls the position of the mouse pointer on the screen. The mouse pointer is usually an arrow shape, but changes depending on the tasks you are performing and the software you are using.

A standard mouse has two buttons. The main mouse operations are *clicking, double-clicking,* and *dragging.*

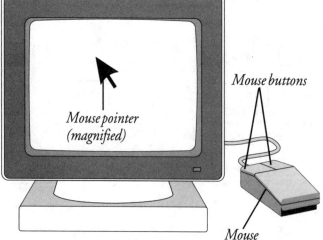

Mouse buttons

Mouse pointer (magnified)

Mouse

PROCESSING

PCs process data through the *central processing unit* (CPU) microchip. It is this device that actually processes the information in the PC.

The CPU follows instructions from the computer's memory to process information. The type of CPU in your PC determines the number and variety of instructions your PC can execute.

Complex tasks performed by your PC are actually a series of simple tasks performed very quickly. The average computer can execute more than two *million instructions per second* (MIPS).

Figure 4. This figure illustrates the Intel 80xx family of CPUs. The first IBM-compatible computers contained the 8088 chip. The 80286 processing chip, when introduced, represented an enormous increase in computing power. Standard PCs now use 80386 and 80486 CPUs.

Intel has now released the successor to the 486 chip, which it calls the Pentium. Many PC vendors will announce products throughout 1993 and 1994 based on this chip.

RAM

Figure 5. *Random access memory* (RAM) primarily stores instructions and data for the immediate use of the CPU. It is called *random access* because the CPU can access information from any part of RAM at any time at random, rather than having to start at the beginning and moving sequentially through to the point you want.

RAM stores data temporarily. You delete the contents of RAM when you switch off, reset, or reboot your computer.

Figure 6. A *byte* is the space approximately one single character occupies in RAM or on disk. Most PCs sold today have at least one megabyte (1 Mb) of RAM. A megabyte is exactly 1,048,576 bytes.

The computer advertised in this figure has 2 Mb of RAM, about two million bytes.

Figure 7. A typical page of text contains about 2,000 characters. A computer with 2 Mb of RAM could, if necessary, store in its RAM the information contained on 1,000 pages.

TYPES OF MEMORY

Figure 8. There are four types of random access memory:

- *Conventional memory*
- *Upper memory*
- *Extended memory*
- *Expanded memory*

If you imagine memory as a stack of blocks, this figure shows how the first three types of RAM stack in your computer's memory.

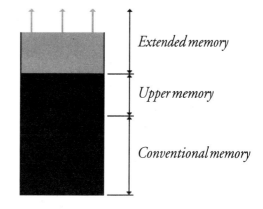

Extended memory

Upper memory

Conventional memory

Figure 9. Conventional memory comprises the first 640 kilobytes (kb) of computer RAM. Generally, most programs use this first 640 kb of RAM only. Even though you may have many megabytes of additional memory installed on your system, you will find a program sometimes runs out of memory because of this 640 kb limitation.

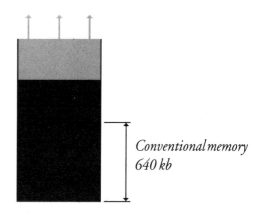

Conventional memory 640 kb

Figure 10. Upper memory is often called reserved memory. It includes the 384 kb of RAM above conventional memory. MS-DOS and the video card that drives your screen use this area of memory.

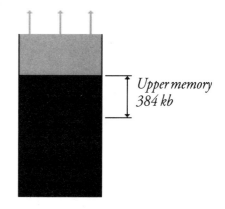

Upper memory 384 kb

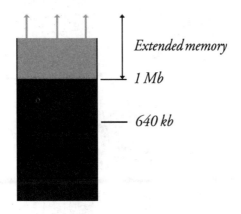

Extended memory

1 Mb

640 kb

Figure 11. Extended memory comprises all memory above the first 1 Mb of your computer's RAM. You may have seen extended memory referred to as XMS (*extended memory specification*).

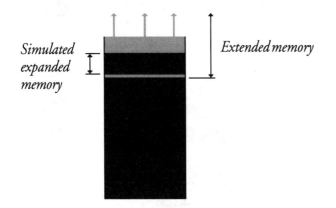

Simulated expanded memory

Extended memory

Figure 12. Originally, expanded memory came as an add-in circuit board to provide early PCs with additional memory. You can configure MS-DOS to use part of extended memory as expanded memory if a program requires it (see **Chapter 9, Customizing Your PC** for more details).

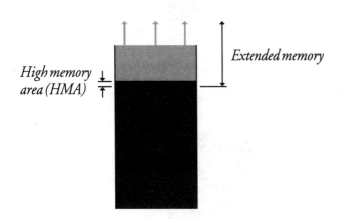

High memory area (HMA)

Extended memory

Figure 13. The *high memory area* (HMA) comprises the first 64 kb of your PC's extended memory. You can get MS-DOS to run in this area of extended memory (see **Chapter 9, Customizing Your PC** for more details).

OUTPUT

The computer needs to provide you with the results of processed data. A device that lets you see processed data is called an "output device."

DISPLAY SCREENS

Figure 14. The screen or monitor is the most common output device for the PC.

Figure 15. The screen connects to particular electronic circuitry inside the computer called a "video adapter," often referred to as a "video card." This card adapts computer signals to a form you can see on the screen.

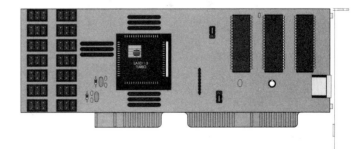

640 x 480 pixels

320 x 200 pixels

Figure 16. The screen displays an image through a series of little dots called "pixels"—or picture elements.

The more pixels displayed on your screen, the greater the resolution. The screen on the left has a resolution of 640 x 480 pixels. The one on the right is lower in resolution, with 320 x 200 pixels.

On a black-and-white (monochrome) screen, a particular pixel is either black (not illuminated) or white (illuminated).

A grayscale monitor, on the other hand, can display a range of grays—up to 256. An image displayed on a grayscale monitor is significantly better in quality than when it is displayed on a monochrome screen.

On a color screen, you can display each pixel as one of a specific range of colors. The number of colors displayed on the screen also determines the quality of an image.

By mixing different amounts of red, green, and blue in one pixel area, a screen can create, in theory, an almost infinite number of colors. This is called RGB technology.

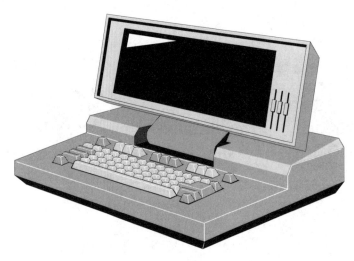

Figure 17. Portable computers use flat screen technology. This is normally plasma, LCD (*liquid crystal display*), or an electroluminescent display.

Portable computers offer built-in monochrome or grayscale screens that can be connected externally to color video screens. Some newer portables now also offer flat screen color displays.

Figure 18. The name of a screen usually reflects the type of video adapter the PC needs to drive it. This table lists the screens in order of resolution (lowest to highest). SVGA screens can show near-photographic resolution.

ACRONYM	FULL NAME
HGC	*Hercules Graphics Card*
MCGA	*Multi-Color Graphics Array*
CGA	*Color Graphics Adapter*
EGA	*Enhanced Graphics Adapter*
VGA	*Video Graphics Array*
SVGA	*Super Video Graphics Array*

PRINTERS

Printers are output devices that let you create a copy of your data on paper. There are two main types of printers: impact and non-impact.

Figure 19. An impact printer strikes the paper with a small piece of metal called a hammer. The printer usually places a ribbon in front of the paper so the hammer leaves a mark.
The most common impact printer is dot matrix. A dot matrix printer creates a character by using certain pins from a matrix (in this example, 24 pins).

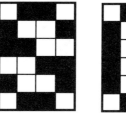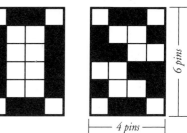

Figure 20. Non-impact printers are much quieter and faster than impact printers. The output is significantly higher in quality. The most common non-impact printers used in business today are laser printers.

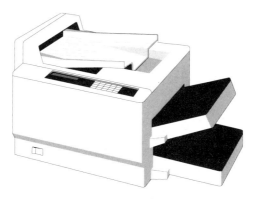

PORTS

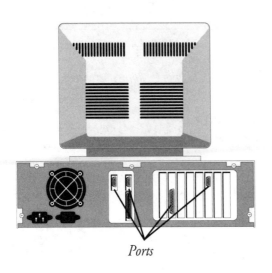

Ports

Figure 21. Ports, or sockets, enable the connection of devices such as keyboards, screens, and printers to a PC. Most ports are at the back of your computer. You communicate data to and from an input or output device through a port.

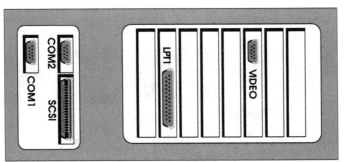

Figure 22. There are several types of ports. Ports often look alike, so most manufacturers label them.

PARALLEL PORTS

PCs usually have a parallel (or LPT1) port. LPT stands for *line printer* as this was once the only device you could plug into a port. If there is more than one parallel port, the PC refers to the others as LPT2, LPT3, and so on.

Opposite ends of a parallel cable

Figure 23. You often use a parallel port to connect a printer to the computer. You use a parallel cable to connect the parallel port on your computer to the parallel port on your printer. The computer can then send data to be printed through this port.

SERIAL PORTS

Most PCs have at least one serial port. People often refer to a serial port as a communications, or COM port. COM1 stands for *communications port 1.* A second port would be called COM2, a third COM3, and so on.

Figure 24. You may have a 9-pin or 25-pin serial port. Both ports operate in exactly the same way.

Figure 25. You can connect a modem, mouse, or printer to your computer through a serial port. A modem lets you communicate with other computers.

You need a serial cable to connect an external device to your PC through the serial port.

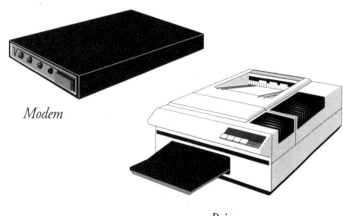

Modem

Printer

SERIAL VERSUS PARALLEL PORTS

The type of printer you have determines the kind of port you connect it to. Some printers connect only to parallel ports and others only to serial. However, you can connect most printers to either. A printer connected to a parallel port usually prints more quickly, because it receives information on eight wires at once, rather than a serial connection's one wire.

You usually connect devices that require two-way communication with a computer—such as a modem—to serial ports.

STORAGE

Because RAM stores data only temporarily, you lose the data when you switch off the computer. To store data permanently, you need a storage device. There are many types of storage devices; the most common are disks.

FLOPPY DISKS

Floppy disks contain one disk platter and a plastic case to protect the surface from damage. Floppy disks come in two sizes: 5¼" and 3½". The sizes refer to the diameter of the disk inside the protective casing. The main advantage of floppy disks is that they are portable.

Write protect notch

Write protect notch

Figure 26. 5¼" disks have a notch on the upper right side called the write-protect notch. When you can see this notch, you can both save files (write) and retrieve files (read) to and from the disk.

When you cover the notch, usually with an adhesive tab, you can no longer write to the disk. This feature is called "write protecting" and it stops you from accidentally modifying or erasing data on a disk.

Figure 27. 3½" disks also have a write-protect notch. It is a small rectangular hole in the upper right of the disk case. A small plastic tab attached to the back of the notch slides back and forth to cover or expose the hole.

When you cover the hole, you can write to and read from the disk. When you open the notch, you write-protect the disk.

Figure 28. You need a floppy disk drive to read from, or write to, floppy disks. A floppy disk drive is a permanent part of your computer system.

As there are two sizes of floppy disks, there are also two sizes of floppy disk drives.

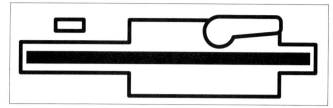

5¼" disk drive

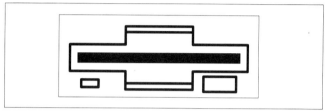

3½" disk drive

Floppy disks have different storage capacities: *double density* and *high density.* Double-density disks hold fewer bytes, or characters. All disk drives can read double-density disks.

High-density disks hold much more data and require a high-density disk drive.

Figure 29. This table shows the storage capacities you have on the different types of floppy disk. The type of disk you use depends on the disk drives in your PC.

	Double Density	High Density
3 $\frac{1}{2}$"	720 kb	1.44 Mb
5 $\frac{1}{4}$"	360 kb	1.2 Mb

HARD DISKS

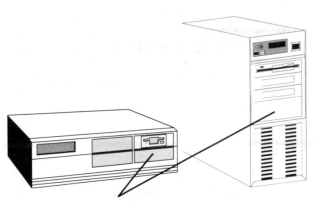

Figure 30. Most PCs have a hard (fixed) disk fitted inside the computer's casing. A hard disk is a permanent part of your computer; it is not portable. Capacities of hard disks vary; 20 Mb is a minimum size and 200 Mb is not uncommon.

The hard disk is inside the computer casing

Hard disks store and retrieve data many times faster than floppy disks.

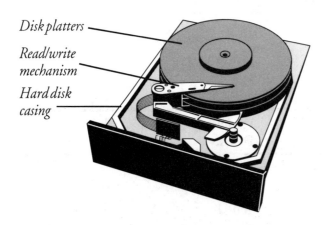

Disk platters

Read/write mechanism

Hard disk casing

Figure 31. A typical hard disk is made up of a number of disk platters. Manufacturers seal the disk platters within a case to prevent damage. They then install the hard disk into the main box of your computer. Once your hard disk is installed, you should not remove it. Trained technicians may remove it for servicing.

The hard disk case contains a mechanism to spin the disks and equipment to read and write data onto the disks.

FORMATTING DISKS

You must format a disk before you can use it to store data. Formatting gives the disk its basic structure. Usually manufacturers format the hard disk before they sell a PC.

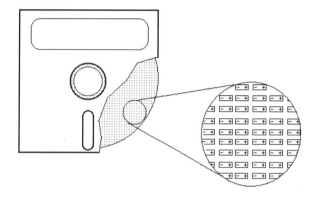

Figure 32. Magnetically sensitive particles cover both hard and floppy disks. When you save a file to disk, the drive head alters the magnetic properties of the disk particles. By reading these patterns, the disk drive can make sense of the information that you have stored on the disk.

DRIVE NAMES

Figure 33. MS-DOS names drives with letters. For example, "C" usually refers to the hard disk in your system. MS-DOS usually calls the floppy disk drive "A;" if you have a second floppy disk drive, MS-DOS calls it "B" in most cases. The drive from which you are currently working is the "current drive."

FILES AND DIRECTORIES

INTRODUCTION

As you use your PC, you begin to accumulate files—the MS-DOS operating system itself consists of about 100 files. A word processing package you install may consist of several hundred files.

You then begin to create letter and document files, which can add significantly to the number of files on your system. It is not unusual for a PC to hold several thousand files.

You can readily access these files if you organize your PC in a systematic way. MS-DOS lets you to do this with directories. This chapter covers basic file organization and directory structure.

Chapter 4, **Command Line Survival** looks at the MS-DOS commands you need to create the structure you want.

Figure 1. When you want to find or store a particular document in your filing cabinet, you have to know what filing cabinet and folder to use. You then put the document in a logical place so you can find it again.

You structure your computer in much the same way as a filing cabinet; just the terms you use are different.

Your filing cabinet is the disk on your PC.

Figure 2. The folder in which you store a document is the equivalent of a disk "directory" in which you store a file on your PC.

Figure 3. The document itself is the equivalent of a "file." Once you know the correct filing cabinet (disk) and folder (directory), it is much easier to find the document (file).

FILE AND DIRECTORY NAMES

You must name every file and directory on your computer, otherwise you couldn't find them. MS-DOS has rules that you must use when naming files and directories.

X
TEMP
CASHBOOK
RESUME
LETTER
LOTUS123

Figure 4. Valid names can be no more than eight characters. Use alphanumeric characters—letters and numbers—in the name. Make sure that you (or one of your colleagues) have not already used the name you now wish to choose, otherwise you replace the existing file with the new one.

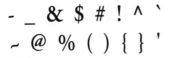

Figure 5. MS-DOS permits some special characters in names. This figure displays a list of special characters that you can use. You cannot use any other special characters in a name.

Figure 6. You cannot use spaces in the name of a directory or file. The invalid name in this example has a space between *NAMES* and *93*. Use a hyphen or underscore to separate words in a name.

Invalid file name

NAMES 93

Valid file names

NAMES_93
NAMES-93

Figure 7. You can add an extension of up to three letters to the end of a name to make it easier to distinguish between files. Use a period (.) to separate the name from the extension.

LETTER.DOC
BUDGET.XLS
CONFIG.SYS
AUTOEXEC.BAT

As a rule, add extensions to files but do not add them to directories. Most programs add a specific extension to the name when you save a file.

FILE TYPES

MS-DOS organizes all data stored on computer disks into a package of information called a "file." There are two main types of files: program files and data files.

PROGRAM FILES

If you want to do anything useful on your computer, you run a program of some kind. Common programs include Microsoft Windows, WordPerfect, and Microsoft Word. People often refer to a computer program as "software" or an "application."

Figure 8. The program includes a series of files which tell the computer how to perform certain tasks. This is similar to following steps in a recipe. Files that make up a program are "program files."

WRITE.HLP
CLOCK.INI
WIN.COM

DATA FILES

A data file usually contains a related group of data, such as a letter, a budget, or a list of client names and addresses. You can create your own data files to store data.

MEMO.DOC

CASHFLOW.WK3

CLIENTS.DB4

Figure 9. The type of file you create depends on the program you're running and what you are doing with it. This figure shows examples of three data files.

The three-character extensions at the end of the file names allow you to distinguish between different types of documents.

DIRECTORIES

Making directories on a disk enables you to find your files easily. You can save time and prevent potential problems by creating an organized directory structure at an early stage.

A well-planned directory system stores files that are:

- **easily found.** Ideally, your knowledge of a file's purpose, and perhaps which application created it, should be enough for you to find and identify it.

- **secure.** You must ensure that you do not accidentally erase, replace, or lose important files.

- **easily backed up.** You need to keep a separate copy of your important files in case your hardware fails or a computer virus infects your PC. Using extensions to identify groups of files allows you to make copies (or backups) of files more easily.

ROOT DIRECTORY

When you format a disk, MS-DOS creates the root directory. This is the base of a directory structure in which you can store files and other directories.

Figure 10. MS-DOS refers to the root directory as a backslash (\ ). On the screen, MS-DOS indicates that you are in the root directory as shown here.

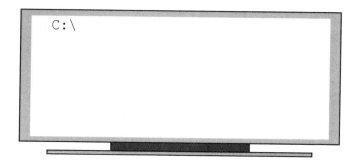

SUBDIRECTORIES

Figure 11. You can include directories within a directory like folders within a folder. You can divide the files in a large directory into a number of smaller directories.

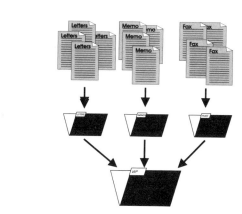

Figure 12. The three directories shown here—*faxes, letters,* and *memos*—let you sort documents in your *wp* directory into smaller, more manageable groups.

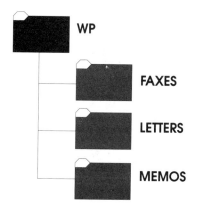

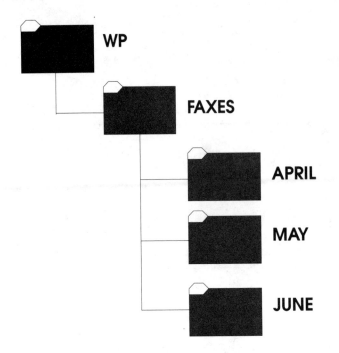

Figure 13. MS-DOS allows you to extend the subdivisions almost indefinitely. This figure shows the *faxes* subdirectory divided into three more subdirectories: *april, may,* and *june.*

With this structure, you would easily find a fax written in May. The file would be in:

- the *wp* subdirectory because you prepared it with a word processor
- the *faxes* subdirectory below *wp* because it is a fax
- the *may* subdirectory below *faxes* as you wrote it in May.

If you wanted to use this directory structure from year to year, then you would copy the faxes from the previous year onto a floppy disk. Removing them from the subdirectory clears the subdirectory for new faxes. **Chapter 4, Command Line Survival** explains how to do this.

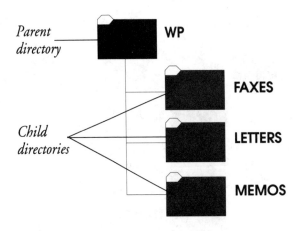

Figure 14. Often people call directories "parent" and "child" directories. The parent is the directory from which the child originates.

DIRECTORY TREE

Figure 15. A directory tree is a visual representation of a disk's directory structure. Many file management programs adopt the directory tree to make working with directories simpler.

This figure depicts a directory tree for a hard disk drive called C:. It contains the first-level directories *database, dos, lotus, sprdshts, wp,* and *word.* We have created subdirectories off most of the directories.

All the directories on the disk have a common root—C:\.

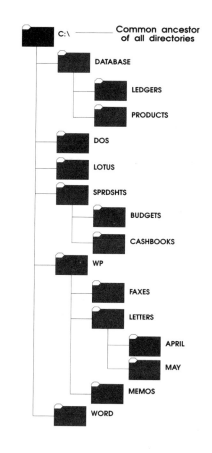

Figure 16. This figure illustrates the *wp* directory as a branch of the directory tree. The *wp* directory is the main branch, subdirectories off that are the smaller branches, and files are the leaves.

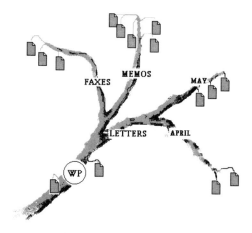

CURRENT DIRECTORY

The current directory is the directory that you have open. MS-DOS always looks for requested files in the current directory.

Figure 17. The root directory is the default current directory when you start your PC. The screen prompt indicates that the current directory is C:\.

PATHNAMES

The "pathname" specifies the exact location of a file in the directory structure. It indicates the directories and subdirectories MS-DOS follows to find the file from the root directory.

The full path to a file begins with the drive letter and the root directory; C:\, for example. It then includes the relevant directories through to the particular file.

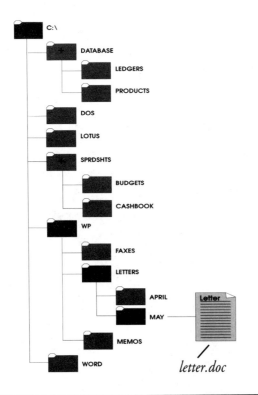

letter.doc

Figure 18. A backslash character (\) separates the directory names. You add the name of the file to the directory path name. The path name of *letter.doc* is *c:\wp\letters\may\letter.doc.*

In this figure, we have indicated in black the directories that form the path to *letter.doc.*

Figure 19. If you use the full path name, MS-DOS can find the file from within any directory, regardless of the current directory.

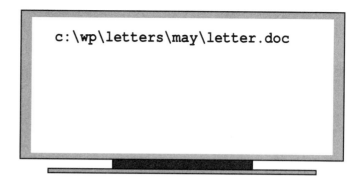

Figure 20. You can omit the drive designator from the path name of the file. MS-DOS assumes that the file is on the current drive.

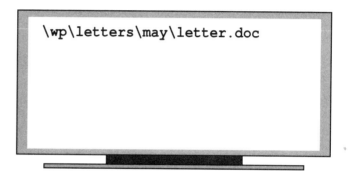

COMMAND LINE SURVIVAL 4

INTRODUCTION

MS-DOS 6 consists of many commands. This chapter concentrates on the commands you need to work with disks, files, and directories.

To help you understand this chapter, all commands and text that you enter are shown in the figures in bold. The information the computer displays is shown in plain text.

ENTERING COMMANDS

Figure 1. To give MS-DOS an instruction, you enter a command at the DOS command prompt. The flashing cursor, indicated by an underscore, is where you enter commands.

```
C:\>_
```

Figure 2. To signal the end of a command, press the Enter key—shown here as <ENTER>.

```
C:\>copy notes.txt b:<ENTER>
```

Figure 3. You can enter MS-DOS commands in upper, lower, or mixed case with the same result.

```
C:\>COPY notes.txt b:\<ENTER>
```

Figure 4. MS-DOS displays an error message if you misspell or enter an unrecognized command. In this case we have misspelled the command *copy* as *copt*.

```
C:\>copt notes.txt b:\
Bad command or file name
```

CHANGING DRIVES

Before DOS executes any commands on your machine, you should find out what the current drive and directory are. You access a disk drive by entering a command containing the appropriate letter. Each disk drive is identified with a letter of the alphabet.

Floppy disk drives are identified by the letters A and B. DOS can use the remaining letters, from C through Z, for any other drives installed on your system: hard disks, RAM disks, CD-ROM drives, network drives, and so on.

Figure 5. The DOS prompt usually reflects the current drive and directory. Here, the DOS prompt shows that drive C is the current drive and the root directory (\) is the current directory.

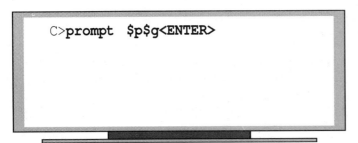

Figure 6. If the DOS prompt on your machine does not reflect the current drive and directory, then entering this prompt command ensures that it does.

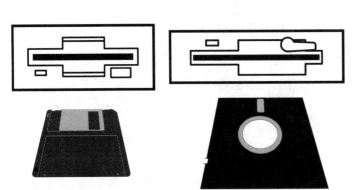

Figure 7. To make drive A the current drive, make sure you have a formatted floppy disk in drive A. Your drive A may be a 3 " or a 5 " floppy disk.

Figure 8. To change to drive A, enter the drive letter "A" (upper or lower case) followed by a colon, then press the Enter key. Drive A becomes the current drive.

```
C:\>a:<ENTER>
A:\>
```

Figure 9. To change back to drive C, enter "C:" then press Enter.

```
A:\>c:<ENTER>
C:\>
```

Figure 10. To change to the B floppy drive, key in "B:"—again, upper or lower case—at the command prompt then press Enter.

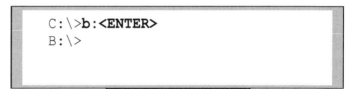

```
C:\>b:<ENTER>
B:\>
```

ERRORS WHEN CHANGING DRIVES

If DOS displays an error message when you try to change drives, you may have one of the problems discussed in Figures 11 through 13.

Figure 11. This means the drive you have selected does not exist on your system.

```
Invalid drive specification
```

Figure 12. You get this message if you haven't inserted a disk into the selected drive. Pressing "A" cancels the operation, "R" retries the drive, and "F" cancels the operation and lets you specify an alternative drive.

```
Not ready reading drive A
Abort, Retry, Fail?
```

Figure 13. This means the drive you have selected contains a disk which is not formatted or is damaged in some way.

```
General error reading drive A
Abort, Retry, Fail?
```

TREE COMMAND

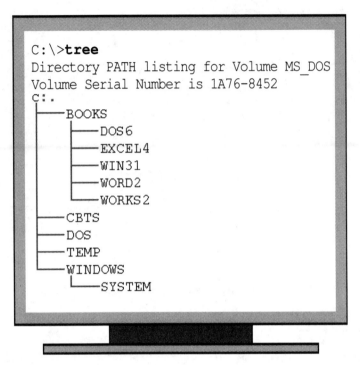

Figure 14. The *tree* command displays all directories in the branch below the current directory (the root directory in this case).

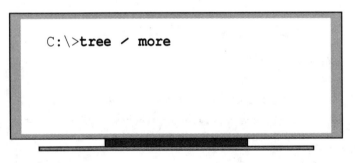

Figure 15. Often the listing scrolls off the screen before you can read it. You can "pipe" the output of the *tree* command to the *more* command. This enables you to read it one screen at a time. **Chapter 8, Advanced Command Techniques** discusses the *more* command in detail.

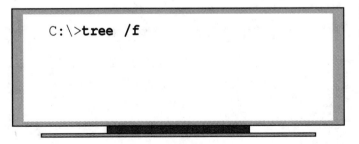

Figure 16. Adding *"/f"* to the *tree* command lists the files in all directories of the current drive.

CHANGING DIRECTORIES

The *cd* (*change directory*) command switches between directories; you key in "cd" and the pathname of the directory to which you want to change.

Figure 17. If the directory is below the current directory, key in a space between *cd* and your required directory.

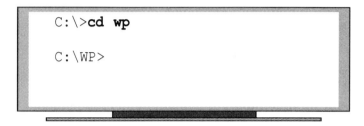

```
C:\>cd wp

C:\WP>
```

Figure 18. You can use the full pathname or the path relative to the current directory. For example, you don't need to key in the full pathname in this case, as *letters\may* is below *wp* in the directory structure.

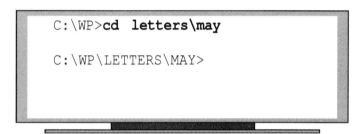

```
C:\WP>cd letters\may

C:\WP\LETTERS\MAY>
```

Figure 19. In this case you need to type in the full pathname (*\wp*) of the *wp* directory because it is above the current directory. The backslash (\) preceding the *wp* directory tells MS-DOS that this is a full pathname, so the search for *wp* starts at the root directory.

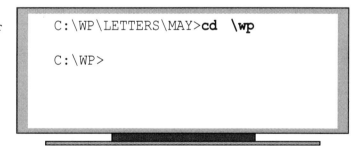

```
C:\WP\LETTERS\MAY>cd \wp

C:\WP>
```

Figure 20. You can use the full pathname to move to a directory in another branch of the tree.

```
C:\WP\>cd \sprdshts\budgets

C:\SPRDSHTS\BUDGETS>
```

```
C:\SPRDSHTS\BUDGETS>cd  ..

C:\SPRDSHTS>
```

Figure 21. MS-DOS always interprets two periods (..) as the parent of the current directory. Typing these in after "cd" takes you to the directory above the current directory.

```
C:\SPRDSHTS\budgets>cd  \

C:\>
```

Figure 22. MS-DOS refers to the root directory with a backslash (\). Keying in a backslash after *cd* returns you to the root directory of the current drive.

```
Invalid  directory
```

Figure 23. MS-DOS displays the error message "Invalid directory" when it cannot find the directory you have specified.

VIEWING DIRECTORIES

Figure 24. The *dir* (*directory*) command lists the contents of the current directory. This figure shows the output of the *dir* command for the directory *c:\wp\letters\may*.

```
C:\WP\LETTERS\MAY>dir

Volume  in drive  C is  MS-DOS
Volume  Serial  Number  is  1728-71FC
Directory  of  C:\WP\LETTERS\MAY

.               <DIR>        04-01-93    2:15p
..              <DIR>        04-01-93    2:15p
LETTER1  DOC    54380        05-03-93    3.52p
LETTER2  DOC     2244        05-11-93    4.26p
LETTER3  DOC     3928        05-12-93    9.28a
     3 file(s)  34793  bytes
               11610  bytes  free
```

The details of this figure are explained below in Figures 25 through 29.

Figure 25. The first three lines of output of the *dir* command show the disk label, serial number, and pathname of the listed directory.

Note: For the remainder of this chapter we leave this information out of directory-listing illustrations.

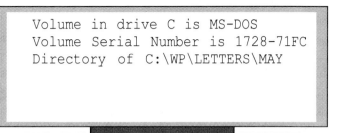

```
Volume in drive C is MS-DOS
Volume Serial Number is 1728-71FC
Directory of C:\WP\LETTERS\MAY
```

Figure 26. The first entry in the *dir* listing, a period (.), refers to the current directory.

```
.              <DIR>        04-01-93    2:15p
```

Figure 27. MS-DOS refers to the parent of the current directory with two periods (..).

Columns to the right show the date and time you created the current directory's parent; in this example: 04-01-93 at 2:15 p.m.

```
..             <DIR>        04-01-93    2:15p
```

Figure 28. Below the directory entries, MS-DOS lists all contained files. It lists file name, file extension, size of the file in bytes, and the date and time you created or last updated the file.

```
LETTER1   DOC      5438   05-03-93    3.52p
LETTER2   DOC      2244   05-11-93    4.26p
LETTER3   DOC      3928   05-12-93    9.28a
```

The list separates the filename and its extension with a space rather than the period it normally uses. The first file in the list, for example, is *letter1*; it has an extension of *doc* and contains 5,438 bytes. We created or updated it on 05-03-93 at 3:52 p.m.

```
      3 file(s)   34793  bytes
                   11610  bytes  free
```

Figure 29. The last lines of the *dir* output show the number of files listed, the total size of the files, and the amount of free space remaining on the current drive.

```
C:\WP\LETTERS\MAY>dir  c:\sprdshts

.               <DIR>      09-10-93    3:22p
..              <DIR>      09-10-93    3:22p
BUDGETS     <DIR>      11-10-93   10:05a
CASHBOOK    <DIR>      11-10-93   10:30a
SALES      DOC   12346  12-10-93   12:05p
```

Figure 30. You can specify a directory's pathname in the *dir* command to list the contents of a directory that is not current. The directory displayed is *sprdshts,* which contains two subdirectories (*budgets* and *cashbook*) and one file (*sales.doc*).

```
C:\WP\LETTERS\MAY>dir  b:\
File  not  found
```

Figure 31. You can list the contents of a directory on another drive by adding the drive specifier to the pathname.

In this example the message indicates that there were no files to be found in the root directory on drive B.

```
C:\SPRDSHTS\BUDGETS>dir  cshflw.xls

CSHFLW    XLS    9323  04-03-93    5:32p
```

Figure 32. You can search for a particular file using the *dir* command. MS-DOS displays its size, and the date and time you created or last updated it.

USING WILDCARDS

The *dir* command often contains files and directories that are of no immediate interest. The names of related files usually contain a pattern.

MS-DOS provides two wildcards so you can use such patterns: the star (*) and the question mark (?). The star substitutes for up to eight characters and the question mark substitutes for just one. You can use wildcard characters to describe the names of the files you want listed with the *dir* command. MS-DOS recognizes wildcard characters in most commands.

Figure 33. In this figure, *dir* lists all files in the current directory. Adding "*.*" to the end of a *dir* command creates the same output, but is superfluous.

```
C:\SPRDSHTS\BUDGETS>dir

MARBDGT    XLS      6222    03-01-93     2:56p
APRBDGT    XLS      5898    04-02-93     4:10p
MAYBDGT    XLS      4392    05-03-93     5:11p
JUNBDGT    XLS      8788    06-04-93     3:10p
JULBDGT    XLS      7532    07-05-93     2:30p
AUGBDGT    XLS     12337    08-06-93     4.32p
TXTRTN     DOC     23456    08-07-93     5:30p
CSHFLW     XLS      8431    08-08-93    11.37a
SEPBDGT    XLS     11986    09-08-93     3.33p
MDCL       DAT      9566    10-08-93     4:28p
```

Figure 34. Replacing the file name with a star (asterisk) and using the *.xls* extension lists all files with the extension *.xls*.

```
C:\SPRDSHTS\BUDGETS>dir  *.xls

MARBDGT    XLS      6222    03-01-93     2:56p
APRBDGT    XLS      5898    04-02-93     4:10p
MAYBDGT    XLS      4392    05-03-93     5:11p
JUNBDGT    XLS      8788    06-04-93     3:10p
JULBDGT    XLS      7532    07-05-93     2:30p
AUGBDGT    XLS     12337    08-06-93     4.32p
SEPBDGT    XLS     11986    09-08-93     3.33p
```

```
C:\>dir auto*.*

AUTOEXEC BAT      337  02-09-93   3:30p
AUTOEXEC DOS      256  03-09-93   1:35p
AUTOEXEC BAK      627  04-05-93  11:29a
AUTOEXEC WIN      445  05-05-93  11:30a
```

Figure 35. In this figure, MS-DOS lists all files with a filename beginning with "*auto.*" We used the star (*) wildcard for the rest of the name and the extension, giving the result as shown.

```
C:\>dir autoexec.ba?

AUTOEXEC BAT      337  02-09-93   3:30p
AUTOEXEC BAK      627  04-05-93  11:29a
```

Figure 36. The question mark (?) substitutes for any single character. In this command, MS-DOS substitutes the "?" wildcard with any valid character.

```
C:\WINDOWS>dir sys???.txt

SYSINI    TXT      408  05-11-93   1:21p
```

Figure 37. Each "?" represents a single character. In this figure, the first three letters of the name must be "*sys,*" but the next three letters can be any valid character.

```
C:\WINDOWS>dir sys???.*
SYSINI    TXT      408  05-11-93   1:21p
SYSINI    BAT      398  06-11-93   1:17p
```

Figure 38. You can mix the two wildcard characters to match more complex patterns.

DIR COMMAND SWITCHES

Figure 39. The */p* (*page*) switch controls long listings that scroll off the screen before you can read them. DOS shows one screen at a time, and you are prompted to press any key when you want to see the next screen.

```
C:\DOS>dir /p

.                 <DIR>         03-08-93    2:15p
..                <DIR>         03-08-93    2:15p
TEXT              <DIR>         03-08-93    4:32p
COUNTRY   SYS      7069         03-10-93    6:00a
EGA       SYS      4885         03-10-93    6:00a
FORMAT    COM     32911         03-10-93    6:00a
KEYB      COM     14986         03-10-93    6:00a
KEYBOARD  SYS     34697         03-10-93    6:00a
NLSFUNC   EXE      7052         03-10-93    6:00a
DISPLAY   SYS     15792         03-10-93    6:00a
HIMEM     SYS     11552         03-10-93    6:00a
MODE      COM     23537         03-10-93    6:00a
SETVER    EXE     12007         03-10-93    6:00a
ANSI      SYS      9029         03-10-93    6:00a
DEBUG     EXE     20634         03-10-93    6:00a
Press any key to continue . . .
```

Figure 40. The */w* (*wide*) switch produces a wide listing across, rather than down, the screen for easier reading. DOS omits the size and date details when you use this switch.

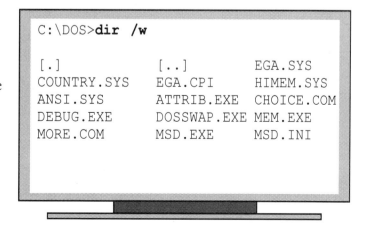

```
C:\DOS>dir /w

[.]               [..]            EGA.SYS
COUNTRY.SYS       EGA.CPI         HIMEM.SYS
ANSI.SYS          ATTRIB.EXE      CHOICE.COM
DEBUG.EXE         DOSSWAP.EXE  MEM.EXE
MORE.COM          MSD.EXE         MSD.INI
```

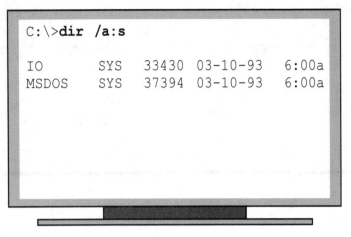

```
C:\>dir /a:s

IO       SYS   33430  03-10-93   6:00a
MSDOS    SYS   37394  03-10-93   6:00a
```

Figure 41. The /a (*attribute*) switch lets you list files with certain attributes, which you specify after the switch. This example uses the /a:s switch to list system files. Other useful combinations using this attribute switch are:

/a:d lists subdirectories.
/a:r lists read-only files.
/a:a lists archive files (files awaiting backup).
/a:h lists hidden files.

```
C:\>dir /o:n

AUTOEXEC BAT     328  04-06-93   2:52p
COMMAND  COM   52925  03-10-93   6:00a
CONFIG   SYS     164  04-06-93   4:20a
DSVXD    386    5741  12-06-93   6:00a
```

Figure 42. The /o switch controls the order of the directory listing. The normal order is by creation date. You can specify these using:

/o:n to list in alphabetical order of file name.
/o:e to list in order of file extension.
/o:s to list in order of file size.
/o:d to list in order of file date.

IDENTIFYING FILES

TIME AND DATE COMMANDS

Often you will find more than one version of the same file in your computer filing system. These files may be duplicates containing the same information, or one file may be more up-to-date than another of the same name. Any filing system, computerized or manual, relies on the correct recording of date and time.

Figure 43. This figure shows a directory of *cshflw.xls* on two different drives. Note the size and date columns—in this case it is likely that the file on drive B is the later version.

```
B:\>dir cshflw.xls

CSHFLW    XLS     8445 12-08-93    2:23p

C:\SPRDSHTS\BUDGETS>dir  cshflw.xls

CSHFLW    XLS     8431 10-08-93  11.37a
```

MS-DOS saves the time and date from the built-in clock for each file when you create or update it.

Some computers do not have a built-in clock, and rely on you to enter the correct date and time when you start up your computer system.

Even if your computer has a built-in clock, you may still need to reset the time and date on occasions.

Figure 44. The *date* command shows the current date and prompts you for a new date. If the command shows the correct date, simply press the Enter key. To change the date, enter the new date in the format indicated.

```
C:\>date
Current date is Wed 03-03-1993
Enter new date (mm-dd-yy):
```

In this example, the required format is *mm-dd-yy*. The format depends on the country setting in your system's *config.sys* file.

Figure 45. The *time* command lets you update the current time. It specifies the format as *hours:minutes:seconds.hundredths of seconds*. The "p" indicates *p.m.;* "a" indicates *a.m.*

```
C:\>time
Current time is 5:58:37.78p
Enter new time:
```

If the time is correct, press the Enter key. If it is not, enter the new time in the same format. MS-DOS does not stop the clock while it prompts you for the new time.

```
C:\>time
Current time is 5:58:37.78p
Enter new time: 6.02p
```

Figure 46. You do not need to enter the new time in the complete format specified. Entering 6.02p sets the time to exactly two minutes past 6 p.m.; you do not have to put in the seconds and hundredths of seconds.

The time is not updated until you press the Enter key; you can, therefore, enter a time in advance, and press the Enter key at exactly that time.

```
Enter new time: 6p
```

Figure 47. You can also leave out the minutes when you enter the new time. You can enter just the hour and "a" or "p" (a.m. or p.m.) when synchronizing the time on the hour.

```
Enter new time: 18
```

Figure 48. The MS-DOS *time* command also accepts 24-hour format. In this figure, we entered 6 p.m. in its corresponding 24-hour format.

VIEWING FILES

One way of identifying files is to view their contents. You can sometimes use the *type* command for this purpose.

```
C:\>cd \dos

C:\DOS>type readme.txt
README.TXT
NOTES ON MS-DOS 6.0
```

Figure 49. The *type* command literally types the contents of text files on the screen, as shown here.

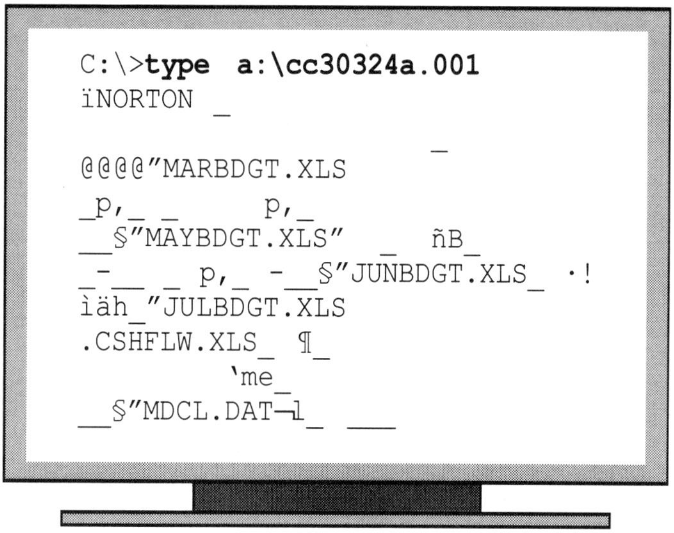

Figure 50. If you use the *type* command to view files other than text files, you won't see much that is recognizable.

```
C:\>type a:\cc30324a.001
ïNORTON _
                          _
@@@@"MARBDGT.XLS
_p,_ _      p,_
__§"MAYBDGT.XLS"    _   ñB_
_-__ _  p,_ -__§"JUNBDGT.XLS_ ·!
ìäh_"JULBDGT.XLS
.CSHFLW.XLS_  ¶_
            'me_
__§"MDCL.DAT¬l_  ___
```

COMPARING FILES

You can use the *fc (file compare)* command to find out if one file is a duplicate of another.

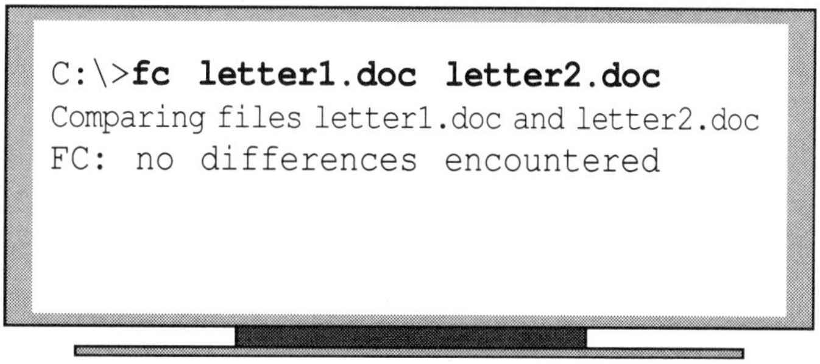

Figure 51. This command compares the contents of *letter1.doc* with *letter2.doc.*

```
C:\>fc letter1.doc letter2.doc
Comparing files letter1.doc and letter2.doc
FC: no differences encountered
```

The *fc* command compares files byte by byte. If the files are not identical, the *fc* command shows where they differ.

NAMING FILES AND DIRECTORIES

RULES

MS-DOS has certain rules for naming files and directories.

```
X
TEMP
CASHBOOK
LETTERS
LOTUS123
```

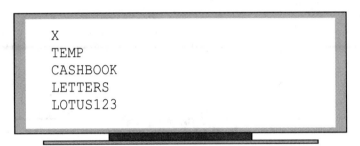

Figure 52. You can use from one to eight characters for a file or directory name.

```
LETTERS.O
LETTERS.OCT
LETTERS.NOV
```

Figure 53. As an option, you can specify an extension of up to three characters after a period.

```
~ ! @ # $ % & _ -
{ } ( )
```

Figure 54. In addition to letters and numbers, you can use these *special characters* in file and directory names. Note that the \, *, ?, and space characters are not permitted in file or directory names. (MS-DOS uses the backslash as the name of the root directory.)

```
@@@.$$$
P&O
SRC-FLS
BGT_MAY
VRSN#1-2-3
```

Figure 55. You can name files and directories with letters, numbers, and special characters.

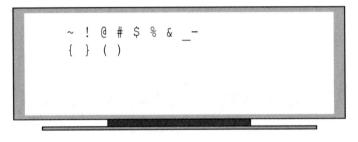

MS-DOS enforces two further rules: you cannot include two files with the same name in a directory, and you cannot have two subdirectories with the same name within the one directory.

FILE EXTENSIONS

Many applications add their own distinctive file extensions to files you create with them.

Figure 56. This figure shows file-name extensions from some popular applications. For example, if you create a document using MS Word and name it *report1*, Word automatically adds the file extension "*doc*."

Application	Extensions Added
MS Word	DOC or DOT
MS EXCEL	XLS or XLM
CorelDraw	CDR
TurboPascal	PAS

These extensions make it easy for you (and the application) to identify files. For this reason, you should not use such extensions for other files.

RENAMING FILES

You will find it easier to identify files if you have a consistent method of naming and sorting them into directories.

Figure 57. This directory structure may be convenient if you write a lot of letters each month.

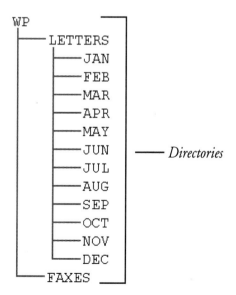

WP
├── LETTERS
│   ├── JAN
│   ├── FEB
│   ├── MAR
│   ├── APR
│   ├── MAY
│   ├── JUN
│   ├── JUL
│   ├── AUG
│   ├── SEP
│   ├── OCT
│   ├── NOV
│   └── DEC
└── FAXES

— *Directories*

```
C:\WP\LETTERS\MAY>dir billy?.doc

BILLY1    DOC   5438  05-03-93   3.52p
BILLY2    DOC   3928  05-05-93   9.28a
```

Figure 58. This directory listing shows that we wrote two letters to *Billy* in May. You need to categorize and rename your files further as you create more.

```
C:\ADIR>ren oldfile.bak newfile.doc
```

Figure 59. The *rename* command lets you specify a new name for a file. This command renames the file *oldfile.bak* as *newfile.doc*.

```
C:\ADIR>ren oldfile2.bak newfile2.doc
Duplicate file name or file not found
```

Figure 60. MS-DOS produced this error message because either it can't find the file *oldfile2.bak* or the file *newfile2.doc* already exists in the current directory. In this case, MS-DOS did not alter the name of the file *oldfile2.bak*.

```
C:\ADIR>ren b:\lib\afile.txt afile.doc
```

Figure 61. If you rename a file in another drive or directory, you must specify its full pathname. This command renames *afile.txt* as *afile.doc*, with the latter file remaining in the directory *b:\lib*.

```
C:\ADIR>ren *.txt *.doc
```

Figure 62. You can use wildcards with the *ren* command. The command in this figure renames all files with the extension *txt* to the extension *doc*.

RUNNING APPLICATIONS

Normally, you would store an application in its own directory. This minimizes the chance that it will be accidentally deleted as you move, update, and delete its document files.

Figure 63. Where possible, you should avoid running an application from its own directory. On one hand you may accidentally overwrite an application system file. You may also find it difficult to identify your own files among the program files.

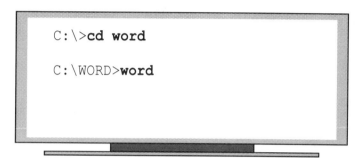

```
C:\>cd word

C:\WORD>word
```

Figure 64. You will find advantages in running applications from the directory containing the documents you wish to edit. When you want to open a document, most applications will show you a list of the documents in the current directory; you simply choose the one you want to use.

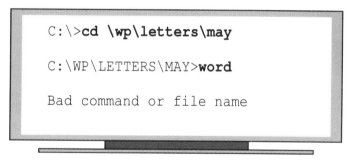

```
C:\>cd \wp\letters\may

C:\WP\LETTERS\MAY>word

Bad command or file name
```

As illustrated in this example, there is a problem: the application itself is not in the current directory, so MS-DOS can't find it.

Figure 65. One way you could overcome the problem in the previous figure is to start an application by specifying its full path name. This generally works—if you can remember where you installed the application.

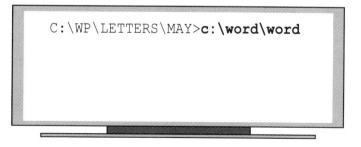

```
C:\WP\LETTERS\MAY>c:\word\word
```

SETTING THE PATH

You can use the *path* command to provide MS-DOS with a way to find your applications.

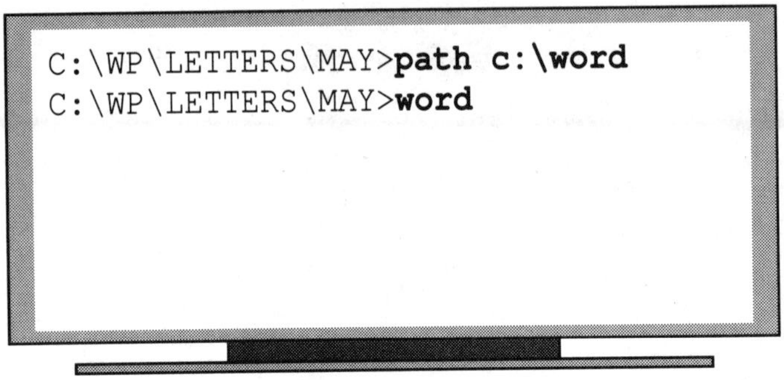

```
C:\WP\LETTERS\MAY>path c:\word
C:\WP\LETTERS\MAY>word
```

Figure 66. For example, you can set the MS-DOS (search) path for the MS-Word program. In this figure, *word.exe* is in the directory *c:\word*. MS-DOS searches the current directory first. If it can't find Word there, it then searches the directory you specify in the *path* command.

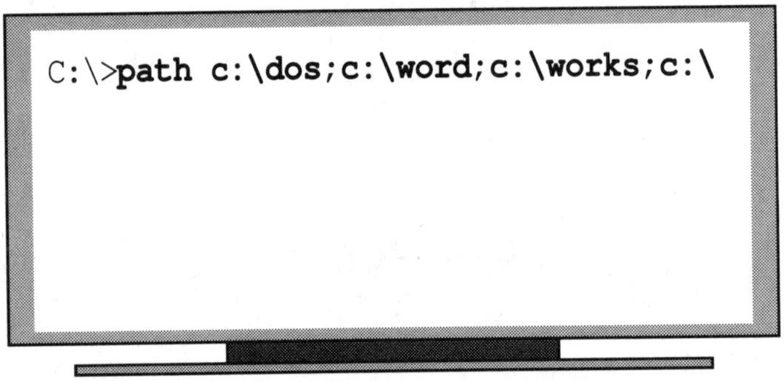

```
C:\>path c:\dos;c:\word;c:\works;c:\
```

Figure 67. You can specify the search path for more than one application. Each path you specify must be separated by a semi-colon (;) and you must not insert any spaces within the command. This example sets paths to the following directories:

1. C:\DOS	so MS-DOS can find its own external commands
2. C:\WORD	so MS-DOS can find the Word program
3. C:\WORKS	so MS-DOS can find the Works program
4. C:	the root directory

Figure 68. You can find the path that you have set by entering the *path* command by itself.

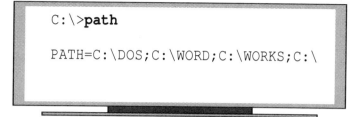

```
C:\>path

PATH=C:\DOS;C:\WORD;C:\WORKS;C:\
```

Figure 69. You should place the *path* command in the *autoexec.bat* file so that MS-DOS automatically sets the path whenever you switch on the computer (see **Chapter 9, Customizing Your PC**). You would normally specify the DOS directory in your path for easy access to the utilities supplied with the operating system.

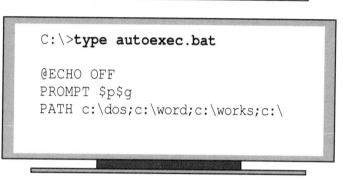

```
C:\>type autoexec.bat

@ECHO OFF
PROMPT $p$g
PATH c:\dos;c:\word;c:\works;c:\
```

MANAGING DIRECTORIES

CREATING DIRECTORIES

You create directories with the *md* (or *mkdir*) command.

Figure 70. If you don't specify a path, the *md* command creates the new directory as a branch or sub-directory of the current directory.

```
C:\>mkdir wp
```

Figure 71. In this figure, we have created the directory *c:\wp\letters*.

```
C:\>cd wp

C:\WP>md letters
```

DELETING DIRECTORIES

With the *rd* command you can delete directories that do not contain files or subdirectories.

```
C:\WP\LETTERS\FEB>del *.*

C:\WP\LETTERS\FEB>cd ..

C:\WP\LETTERS>rd feb
```

Figure 72. The first command in this figure deletes all files in the directory. The second command logs into the parent directory, and the third deletes the directory. Note that you cannot delete the current directory.

```
C:\WP\LETTERS>rd b:\notes
```

Figure 73. As with all MS-DOS commands, you can use path-names with the *rd* command. The command shown in this figure removes the directory *\notes* on drive B, if it does not contain any files or subdirectories.

The *deltree* command lets you remove a directory without having to delete all its files and subdirectories first.

```
C:\WP\LETTERS>deltree feb
Delete directory "feb" and all its
subdirectories? [yn]

Deleting feb...
```

Figure 74. The *deltree* command gives you the same result as the sequence of commands shown in Figure 72. The *deltree* command removes all the files and subdirectories in the specified directory. Deltree prompts you for each file and subdirectory it deletes under the directory you specify.

FILE MANAGEMENT

COPYING FILES

You use the *copy* command to copy a file or group of files.

The file you are copying is called the *source* file. The copy of this file is called the *destination* file. In some situations data is overwritten in the copying process. This is demonstrated in some of the following examples.

Figure 75. In this example, we:

1. use the *cd* command to log into the directory containing the file to copy;
2. confirm the names of the files using the *dir* command;
3. copy *lett1.doc* to *lett3.doc*; and
4. use the *dir* command to check whether the copy operation was successful.

Note that the size and date stamp of the destination file *lett3.doc* is identical to the source file *lett1.doc*.

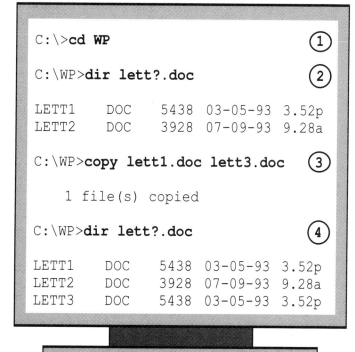

```
C:\>cd WP                              (1)

C:\WP>dir lett?.doc                    (2)

LETT1    DOC    5438   03-05-93  3.52p
LETT2    DOC    3928   07-09-93  9.28a

C:\WP>copy lett1.doc lett3.doc         (3)

     1 file(s) copied

C:\WP>dir lett?.doc                    (4)

LETT1    DOC    5438   03-05-93  3.52p
LETT2    DOC    3928   07-09-93  9.28a
LETT3    DOC    5438   03-05-93  3.52p
```

Figure 76. You may find it easier to copy files from the current directory. However, if you enter the command shown here from the root directory, it produces exactly the same results as in Steps 1 and 3 of Figure 75.

```
C:\>copy \wp\lett1.doc \wp\lett3.doc

     1 file(s) copied
```

```
C:\WP>dir lett?.doc

LETT1     DOC     5438   03-05-93    3.52p
LETT2     DOC     3928   07-09-93    9.28a
LETT3     DOC     5438   03-05-93    3.52p

C:\WP>copy lett1.doc lett2.doc

    1 file(s) copied

C:\WP>dir lett?.doc

LETT1     DOC     5438   03-05-93    3.52p
LETT2     DOC     5438   03-05-93    3.52p
LETT3     DOC     5438   03-05-93    3.52p
```

Figure 77. If there is already a file with the name you gave your destination file, then the *copy* command overwrites it with the source file. In this figure, the *copy* command replaces the file *lett2.doc* with a copy of *lett1.doc*; the system overwrites the original *lett2.doc* document.

```
C:\WP>copy lett?.doc c:\files

    3 file(s) copied

C:\WP>dir c:\files

LETT1     DOC     5438   03-05-93    3.52p
LETT2     DOC     5438   03-05-93    3.52p
LETT3     DOC     5438   03-05-93    3.52p
```

Figure 78. If you omit the name of the destination file, the new file will have the same name as the source file. Unless you want to rename the destination file in the process, you need to specify its path only.

Figure 79. You can use wildcards to copy a group of files. In this case, MS-DOS copies the files to drive B. You can use this method to backup groups of files, or to make copies of multiple files with one command.

```
C:\WP>dir le*.doc

LETT1     DOC     5438  03-05-93   3.52p
LETT2     DOC     5438  03-05-93   3.52p
LETT3     DOC     5438  03-05-93   3.52p
LETTER    DOC     3928  08-06-93   9.28a
LESTWE    DOC     4877  10-11-93  11.22a

C:\WP>copy le*.doc b:\
    5 file(s) copied

C:\WP>dir b:\

LETT1     DOC     5438  03-05-93   3.52p
LETT2     DOC     5438  03-05-93   3.52p
LETT3     DOC     5438  03-05-93   3.52p
LETTER    DOC     3928  08-06-93   9.28a
LESTWE    DOC     4877  10-11-93  11.22a
```

Figure 80. This figure shows how to copy a series of documents in the current directory to drive B. The wildcard character ensures that MS-DOS copies all files with the extension "*doc.*"

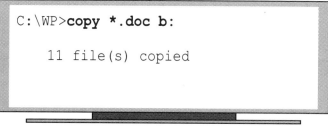

```
C:\WP>copy *.doc b:

    11 file(s) copied
```

The second command in this figure copies all files in the current directory to another drive. We left out the directory path of the source files, so the current directory is the default. We also left out the destination directory, so the current directory on the B drive is the default.

```
C:\WP\LETTERS\MAY>copy *.* b:

    17 file(s) copied
```

```
C:\WP>copy b:*.* c:
```

Figure 81. This command copies all files in the current directory of drive B to the current directory (*wp*) of the C drive.

DELETING FILES

You use the *del* (*delete*) command to delete files.

```
C:\WP>del lett20.doc
File not found
```

Figure 82. If you try to delete a file that does not exist, MS-DOS replies with the error message shown in this figure.

```
C:\WP>del video.sys
Access denied
```

Figure 83. Trying to delete a protected file displays the error message shown. (See later in this chapter on how to protect files.)

```
C:\WP\LETTERS\MAY>dir billy*.doc

BILLY1   DOC   5438  05-03-93   3.52p
BILLY2   DOC   3928  05-05-93   9.28a
BILLYBOY DOC   4877  05-07-93  11.22a

C:\WP\LETTERS\MAY>del billy*.doc
```

Figure 84. You can use wildcards to delete a group of files, but you should make sure you check the files first. Do this by using the same filename, including the wildcards, with the *dir* command.

```
C:\WP\WP\LETTERS\MAY>del *.*
```

Figure 85. This command deletes all files in the current directory. Be careful when using this command with wildcards. It can have devastating results if you use it incorrectly (using it in the root directory, for example).

UNDELETING FILES

You may, on occasion, delete a file or a group of files by mistake. However, you can sometimes recover deleted files using the *undelete* command. If you use the *undelete* command immediately after you delete something, you increase your chances of recovering it. Once you have saved a file into the space occupied by the deleted files, you cannot retrieve them.

Figure 86. MS-DOS asks you for the first letter of the file name if it can recover the file.

```
C:\WP\LETTERS\MAY>undelete billy1.doc

Please type the first character for ?ILLY1.DOC:
```

Figure 87. You can use wildcards with the *undelete* command to recover a group of files.

```
C:\WP\LETTERS\MAY>del *.*

C:\WP\LETTERS\MAY>undelete *.*
```

MOVING FILES

The *move* command copies and deletes in a single action.

Figure 88. The commands shown in this figure copy the file *billy1.doc* from the *letters* directory to the *temp* directory and delete *billy1.doc* from the *letters* directory. We are using the *copy* and *del* commands to move a file from one directory to another.

```
C:\WP\LETTERS>copy billy1.doc temp

    1 file(s) copied

C:\WP\LETTERS>del billy1.doc
```

```
C:\WP\LETTERS>move billy1.doc temp
c:\wp\letters\billy.doc => c:\temp [ok]
```

Figure 89. The *move* command lets you use the *copy* and *del* shown in Figure 88 in one action. *Move* not only copies the file from the *letters* directory to the *temp* directory, it also deletes the original file in the process.

*Note: When you move files on the same drive, the move command helps prevent files from becoming fragmented (see **Chapter 7, In Charge of Your System**). This is because only the file's directory path is altered and the file is not actually physically relocated on the disk.*

PROTECTING FILES

Figure 90. Every file has four attributes. Attributes are like switches, because you can turn them on (set) or off (cleared).

Attribute	Effect When Set
Read-Only r	You cannot delete or alter the contents of read-only files but you can copy, print, or view them.
Hidden h	A hidden file is invisible to all MS-DOS commands except dir and attrib.
System s	The system attribute provides the same level of protection as the Hidden attribute, but is intended for use only by MS-DOS.
Archive a	The archive attribute indicates that you have updated a file since you last archived it. (See the following section on Archiving Data.)

```
C:>\SPRDSHTS\BUDGETS>attrib +r cshflw.xls
```

Figure 91. This figure shows how you can protect the file *cshflw.xls* by setting (+) the *read-only attribute* (r). The read-only attribute protects the file and stops you from deleting or updating it.

Figure 92. This first command in this figure shows how to clear (-) the read-only attribute. You can now delete or update this file.

```
C:>\SPRDSHTS\BUDGETS>attrib -r cshflw.xls
```

You can use wildcards to set (or clear) attributes for multiple files in one operation. The second command in this figure sets the archive and read-only attributes for all files with the extension *xls*. Note that you must leave a space between each attribute listed in the command.

```
C:>\SPRDSHTS\BUDGETS>attrib +a +r *.xls
```

Figure 93. You can use the *attrib* command to check the attributes of a file. In this case we have previously set the archive and read-only attributes for the *cshflw.xls* file. Note the A and R at the beginning of the line.

```
C:>\SPRDSHTS\BUDGETS>attrib cshflw.xls
A R C:\SPRDSHTS\BUDGETS>CSHFLW.XLS
```

Figure 94. You can also use wildcards to check the attributes of a group of files.

```
C:>\SPRDSHTS\BUDGETS>attrib *.xls
A R C:\SPRDSHTS\BUDGETS>AUGBDGT.XLS
A R C:\SPRDSHTS\BUDGETS>CSHFLW.XLS
A R C:\SPRDSHTS\BUDGETS>SEPBDGT.XLS
```

Figure 95. We have used the *attrib* command in this figure to set the hidden attributes for the group of files *.xls*. The *dir* command reports that it cannot find the files, because we have hidden them.

```
C:>\SPRDSHTS\BUDGETS>attrib +h *.xls
C:>\SPRDSHTS\BUDGETS>dir *.xls
File not found
```

```
C:>\SPRDSHTS\BUDGETS>dir *.xls /ah

AUGBDGT   XLS    12337  08-06-93    4.32p
CSHFLW    XLS     8431  08-08-93   11.37a
SEPBDGT   XLS    11986  09-08-93    3.33p
          3 file(s)
```

Figure 96. You use the */ah (attribute hidden)* switch with the *dir* command to list hidden files. The *dir* command is the only other DOS command that can "see" hidden files.

```
C:>\SPRDSHTS\BUDGETS>attrib -h *.xls

C:>\SPRDSHTS\BUDGETS>dir *.xls

AUGBDGT   XLS    12337  08-06-93    4.32p
CSHFLW    XLS     8431  08-08-93   11.37a
SEPBDGT   XLS    11986  09-08-93    3.33p
          3 file(s)
```

Figure 97. This figure shows how to clear the hidden attribute of a group of files so that MS-DOS commands can "see" them.

USING XCOPY

The *xcopy* command has two switches that make it an excellent copying tool.

```
C:>\SPRDSHTS\BUDGETS>xcopy c: a:   /m
Reading source file(s) ...
C:MARBDGT.XLS
C:APRBDGT.XLS
C:MAYBDGT.XLS
C:JUNBDGT.XLS
C:JULBDGT.XLS
C:AUGBDGT.XLS
C:CSHFLW.XLS
C:SEPBDGT.XLS
         8 File(s) copied
```

Figure 98. You can use the */m (modify attribute)* switch with the *xcopy* command to copy files that have changed only since you last archived them. The *xcopy* command also clears the archive attribute of source files to show that you have archived them.

In this figure, we're copying all files in the current directory with the archive attribute to drive A.

Figure 99. In this figure we have used the *dir* command with the /*aa* (*attribute archive*) switch to list the files that have altered since you last archived them. We have then used the *xcopy* command with the /*m* switch to copy only these files to drive A.

```
C:>\SPRDSHTS\BUDGETS>dir *.* /aa
AUGBDGT   XLS    12337  08-06-93     4.32p
CSHFLW    XLS     8431  08-08-93    11.37a
SEPBDGT   XLS    11986  09-08-93     3.33p

C:>\SPRDSHTS\BUDGETS>xcopy c: a:   /m
Reading source file(s)
C:AUGBDGT.XLS
C:CSHFLW.XLS
C:SEPBDGT.XLS
            3 File(s) copied.
```

Figure 100. Specify the /*s* option to copy files in the *wp* directory and its subdirectories to drive A. *Xcopy* creates the subdirectory names on the destination drive as part of the copy process.

```
C:\>xcopy wp a: /s
Reading source file(s) ...
WP\MAIL.DOC
WP\LETTERS\FEB\CLIENTS.DOC
WP\LETTERS\MAR\BILLY1.DOC
```

PRINTING FILES

You can use the *print* command to print text files. Line up a group of files for printing and add files to this queue as needed. The printing process goes on in the background, so you can use the computer for other purposes.

Figure 101. When you initiate the *print* command, you are prompted for the name of the *list device*. The default output device (PRN) is suitable in most cases, so you can just press the Enter key. Check your printer if it doesn't start printing immediately.

```
C:\>print config.sys
Name of list device [PRN]: _
```

```
C:\>print c:\txtdir\*.txt /p
```

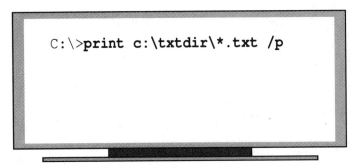

Figure 102. You can use wildcards to queue files for printing. If the printer is currently printing a file, use the */p* switch to add more files to the print queue.

```
C:\>print
C:\CONFIG.SYS
C:\TXTDIR\FILE1.TXT
C:\TXTDIR\FILE2.TXT
C:\TXTDIR\FILE3.TXT
```

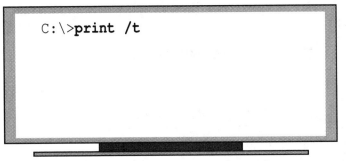

Figure 103. To list the files in the print queue, enter the *print* command without any parameters.

```
C:\>print /t
```

Figure 104. You can clear the print queue using the */t* switch.

Disk Management

Formatting a Disk

Most disks, when you buy them, are not formatted. The formatting process prepares a disk for use with MS-DOS. Before you format a disk, make sure it that it is either a brand new disk, or that it does not contain any valuable information.

Figure 105. To format a floppy disk, put it in the A or B drive, depending on the type of disk and the number of floppy drives your system uses. Type "format" and the name of the drive where you put the floppy disk.

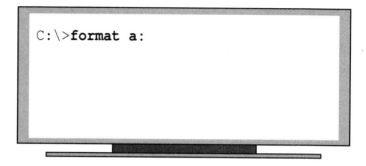

Figure 106. *Format* shows you its progress as it prepares the disk.

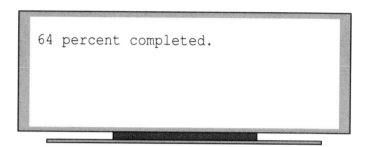

Figure 107. When *Format* completes the process, it offers you the chance to give the formatted disk a name, called a label. You can either enter a description of up to eleven characters or bypass the step by just pressing Enter. After it has done this, *Format* asks if you want to format another disk.

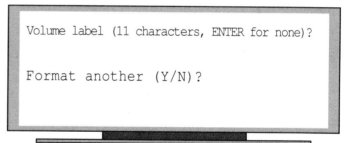

Figure 108. If you wish to format a disk as a system disk (a disk that contains the operating system), type the command shown here.

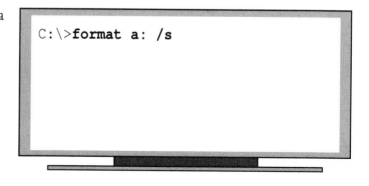

UNFORMATTING A DISK

You may notice the message "Saving UNFORMAT information" when formatting a disk. The *Unformat* command uses this unformat information when you recover the contents of a formatted disk. You must use the *Unformat* command with care as you can lose data if you accidentally do it on the wrong disk.

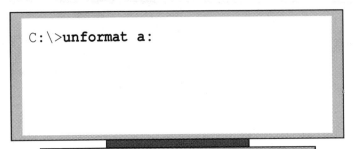

```
C:\>unformat a:
```

Figure 109. Type "unformat" and the letter of the drive where you put the disk.

```
Are you sure you want to update the
system area of your drive A (Y/N)?
```

Figure 110. *Unformat* asks you if you want to continue.

The unformat process will be successful as long as you did not write anything to the disk, such as copying a file to it, which may have overwritten data.

DISK COPYING

With the *diskcopy* command, you can copy the contents of one floppy disk to another. You can use the *diskcopy* command only on floppy disks. If the destination disk is not formatted, then *diskcopy* will format it as it copies.

Figure 111. If you have two floppy disk drives (A and B), you can put the source disk in the A drive and the destination disk in the B drive, and enter this command.

```
C:\>diskcopy a: b:

Insert SOURCE diskette in drive A:
Insert TARGET diskette in drive B:

Press any key to continue . . .
```

Figure 112. *Diskcopy* also caters for single floppy drive systems. Place the source disk in drive A, and *diskcopy* prompts you to change disks each time it needs to write to the destination disk.

```
C:\>diskcopy a: a:

Insert SOURCE diskette in drive A:

Press any key to continue . . .
```

DISK COMPARING

As with the *diskcopy* command, you can compare disks using a single or twin floppy drive system. You can compare the contents of floppy disks only. See the *fc* command earlier in this chapter if you want to compare files on a disk.

Figure 113. Insert the first disk into drive A and enter the command shown if you only have one floppy disk drive. *Diskcomp* prompts you to change disks during the operation.

```
C:\>diskcomp a: a:

Insert FIRST diskette in drive A:

Press any key to continue . . .
```

Figure 114. *Diskcomp* reports whether the two disks are identical and prompts you if you want to compare another disk.

```
Compare OK
Compare another diskette <Y/N> ?
```

DETECTING ERRORS

The chkdsk *(check disk) command gives you information about a disk and checks the filing system tables to make sure they do not contain any errors.*

```
C:\>chkdsk
Volume MS-DOS created 07-29-1993 5:12p
Volume Serial Number is 2A6C-15DE

121290752 bytes total disk space
     7328 bytes in 2 hidden files
   215040 bytes in 89 directories
113670144 bytes in 2339 user files
  7620608 bytes available on disk

     2048 bytes in each allocation unit
    59224 total allocation units on disk
     3580 available allocation units on disk

   655360 total bytes memory
   577520 bytes free
```

Figure 115. The *chkdsk* command displays a status report giving you statistics about disk space and random access memory. If you leave out the drive letter from the command, it assumes the current drive.

```
1 lost allocation units found in 1 chains.
  2048 bytes disk space would be freed
```

Figure 116. The *chkdsk* command can identify file system errors. A file consists of a number of allocation units, much like a chain is made up of individual links. When this command reports an allocation unit as "lost," you may find that the system has damaged one of your files.

If you use a damaged or corrupted file, you can create serious problems in the file system, which may result in failure of the operating system.

Figure 117. You can use the */f (fix)* switch to allow *chkdsk* to correct file linkage problems.

```
C:\>chkdsk /f
```

Figure 118. You can sometimes identify the damaged files if you enter *Y* (for yes) to the question shown in this figure. *Chkdsk* writes the contents of the lost allocation units as files in the root directory for you to inspect.

```
1 lost allocation units found in 1 chains.
Convert lost chains to files? (Y/N)
```

Figure 119. *Chkdsk* writes a file for each chain of lost units. You can check the contents of such a file with the *type* command.

```
C:\>dir file000?.chk
FILE0001 CHK      4096  02-09-93  12:32p
FILE0002 CHK     12288  02-09-93  12:32p
FILE0003 CHK      6144  02-09-93  12:32p

C:\>type file0001.chk
```

Note: Run chkdsk *on a regular basis, especially after a program crash or a power failure. Often these incidents occur while the operating system is updating files, so naturally data is lost and files are left in disarray.*

MS-DOS Shell [5]

Introduction

Learning and using the command line is a complex and time-consuming task. You must remember commands, file names, and switches when using the MS-DOS command line to manage files. The Shell, by contrast, is a visual and intuitive tool.

Starting the Shell

You can configure your system to load the Shell automatically when you start your PC (see **Chapter 9, Customizing Your PC**) or you can start it from the command line.

Figure 1. Type "dosshell" at the command line to start the Shell.

```
C:\>dosshell
```

Figure 2. The Shell begins by scanning the directory tree of the current drive.

```
Reading Disk Information . . .

Files Read:              248
Directories Read:         30
```

To print files from the Shell, you need to run the DOS Print program before starting the Shell. Refer to **Printing Files** later in this chapter.

SHELL SCREEN

Figure 3. The default Shell screen windows display in graphics mode. The Shell, however, does offer text modes suitable for MDA and CGA adapters.

Figures 4 through 8 describe the major components of the Shell screen.

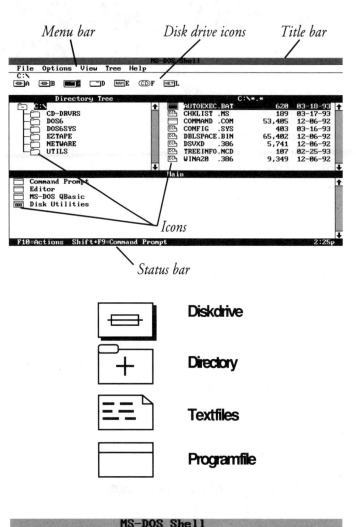

Menu bar   Disk drive icons   Title bar

Icons

Status bar

Diskdrive

Directory

Textfiles

Programfile

Figure 4. The Shell shows files, programs, directories, and disk drives as objects called icons.

Clicking, double-clicking, and dragging icons with the mouse allows you to do many tasks quickly and easily. However, the mouse is not essential; you can do most things without it.

MS-DOS Shell

Figure 5. The title bar identifies the current application. It is especially useful when you move between applications.

File   Options   View   Tree   Help

Figure 6. The Shell menu bar shows the menus you can select. The list of menus can vary, depending on the Shell screen area in which you are working.

Figure 7. Disk drive icons represent the installed disk drives.

In this example, the system has two floppy drives (A and B), a hard disk (C), another hard disk (D), a RAM disk (E), a CD-ROM disk (F), and a network disk drive (L). Here the Shell is highlighting the icon for drive C, indicating that it is the current drive. You can make another drive current by selecting its icon or using the arrow keys.

Figure 8. The Shell status bar displays hints and messages.

```
F10=Actions   Shift+F9=Command Prompt
```

WORKING WITH THE SHELL

SCREEN AREAS

Figure 9. The Shell divides the screen into the five areas indicated in this figure. Each of the *List* areas (*Directory Tree, File, Program,* and *Active Task*) has a title bar. When you activate a list area, the Shell highlights its title bar. The selected item in the list box is the selection cursor.

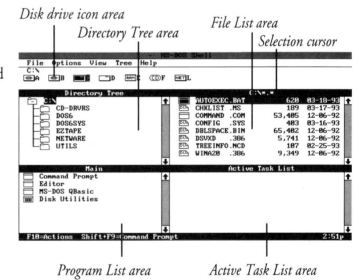

Figure 10. The *Directory Tree* area displays the directory of the current drive. The highlighted directory name "*personal*" indicates that it is the current directory.

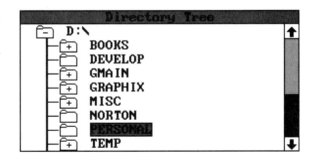

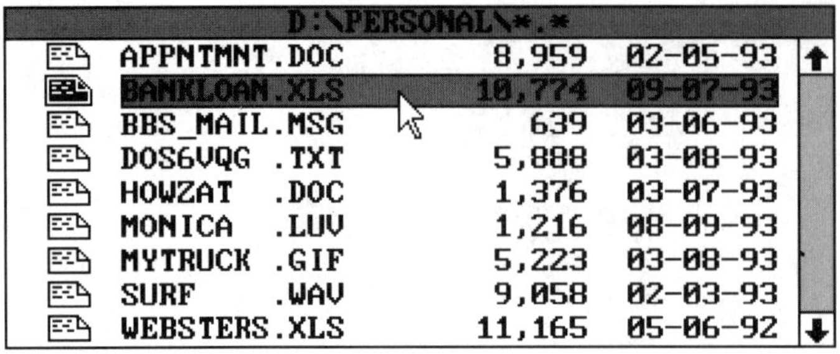

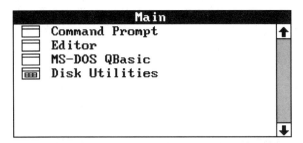

Figure 11. The *File List* area shows the names of the files in the current directory. The title bar indicates the name of the current directory. In graphics mode, it also shows icons representing the type of files as seen here.

In this figure the selected file is ***bankloan.xls***. The Shell highlights both the file name and icon.

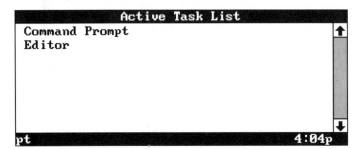

Figure 12. Selecting *Program/File Lists* in the **View** menu displays the *Program List*. By default, the Shell displays the Main group, as shown here. You can put your most frequently used applications into the *Program List* so that you can access them easily.

Figure 13. Choose the *Enable Task Swapper* command from the **Options** menu to see the *Active Task List*. In this example, the *Active Task List* window shows that we are running the Editor and the Command Prompt. The Shell is the current application.

CHANGING THE ACTIVE SHELL AREA

MOUSE

Click on the area you want.

KEYBOARD

Tab

Figure 14. Press the Tab key until you select the area you want.

SELECTING AN OBJECT IN THE SHELL

MOUSE

Click on the icon you want.

KEYBOARD

Figure 15. Press the Tab key until you activate the area you want and then use the Arrow keys to position the selection cursor over the required icon.

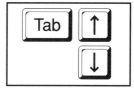

MENUS

This section discusses methods of selecting menu commands within the Shell.

MENU CHARACTERISTICS

Figure 16. If you click on the word File in the menu bar of the MS-DOS Shell, the menu drops down to show the commands. The name of the highlighted command is the **File**/*Open* command, because it is the *Open* command in the **File** menu.

   Figure 17 on the next page describes the different options and features contained in this and similar menus.

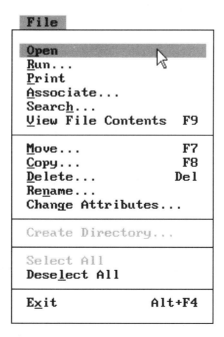

Figure 17. The table below explains the different characteristics of a menu (in this case the **File** menu). Similar features are available in all other Shell menus.

Feature	Commands	Explanation
Accelerator keys	Open	The underscored letter in each command name provides accelerated access to the command, after opening the menu.
Shortcut keys	Exit Alt+F4	Entering the key (combination) to the right of the command selects the command directly, without opening the menu.
Ellipsis	Run...	An ellipsis following a command indicates that it leads to a dialog box. You enter the information necessary to complete the command in the dialog box.
Dimmed commands	Create Directory	Dimmed commands are temporarily unavailable for some reason (in this case, because the Directory Tree window is not selected).

OPENING A MENU

MOUSE

`File    Options    View`

Figure 18. Click on the menu name to open that menu.

KEYBOARD

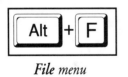

File menu

Figure 19. Press the Alt key and the Shell displays an underscore under the first letter in each menu name. Press the underscored letter representing the menu you want. For example, to open the **File** menu, press Alt then F.

CLOSING A MENU

MOUSE

Figure 20. Click on the menu name again or, to avoid accidentally selecting another command, you can click on the right side of the menu bar.

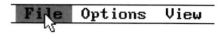

KEYBOARD

Figure 21. Press the Esc or the Alt key.

INVOKING A MENU COMMAND

MOUSE

Figure 22. Open the appropriate menu, then click on the command you want.

KEYBOARD

Figure 23. Open the appropriate menu and press the underlined letter for the command.

OR

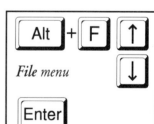

File menu; Open command

Open the appropriate menu and press the Down Arrow or Up Arrow key until the selection cursor highlights the command you want, then press the Enter key.

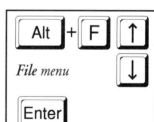

OR

Type the shortcut for the command shown. For example, press the Asterisk key to expand a branch of the directory.

GETTING HELP

MOUSE

For general help, choose the relevant command from the
Help menu.

KEYBOARD

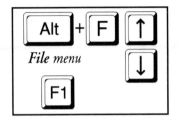

Alt + F
File menu
↑ ↓
F1

Figure 24. Open the appropriate menu and select the command you want, then press the F1 key.

A dialog box appears providing information on the selected
command.

DIALOG BOXES

Dialog boxes provide a way for you to specify additional information for a particular command.

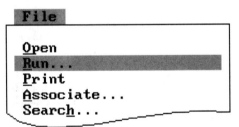

File

Open
Run...
Print
Associate...
Search...

Figure 25. The ellipsis (...) alongside the command name indicates
that the command displays a dialog box in which you provide this
additional information.

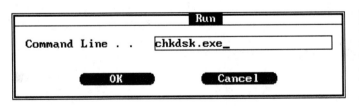

Run

Command Line . . chkdsk.exe_

OK   Cancel

Figure 26. When you select the
File/*Run* command, the Shell
opens the *Run* dialog box. Once
you have entered the name of the
program into the dialog box, click
on *OK.*

CUSTOMIZING THE SHELL

The Shell has three text display modes and five graphics display modes. You can only access these latter modes if your monitor supports graphics. With this exception, you can choose whichever mode suits you.

The Shell also supports several color schemes. Naturally, the different color schemes are relevant only if your monitor can display color.

Figure 27. The **Options** menu contains the *Display* and *Colors* commands. These commands enable you to change the appearance of the screen.

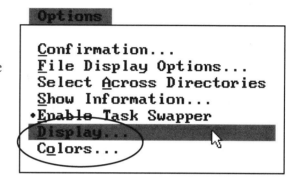

WORKING WITH DIRECTORIES

Almost everything you do with the Shell involves finding and displaying one or more directories. The Shell provides excellent facilities for doing this.

Figure 28. The *Directory Tree* area below shows the directory tree on drive D. The current directory is *D:\general\personal* and the Shell lists the names of its files in the *File List* area.

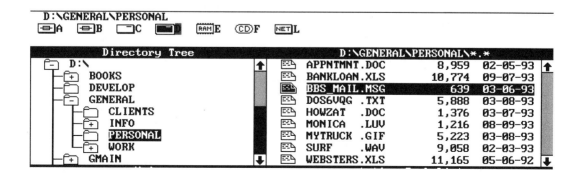

SELECTING A DIRECTORY

When you start the Shell, it displays the files in the root directory of the current drive. However, you sometimes need to work with files on another drive.

CHANGING THE CURRENT DRIVE

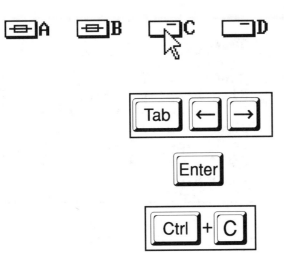

MOUSE

Figure 29. Click on the icon for the required drive.

KEYBOARD

Figure 30. Press the Tab key until you have highlighted the current drive icon. Then use the Left Arrow or Right Arrow key to select the new drive icon, and press the Enter key.

Alternatively, you can also hold down the Control key and press the key for the drive letter. For example, if you press Ctrl+C, this selects the C drive.

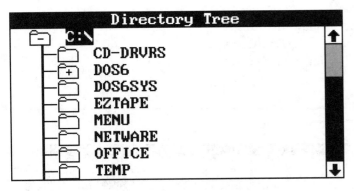

Figure 31. The Shell displays the directory tree for the selected drive in the *Directory Tree* area.

To display a particular directory, you may need to do one or more of the following:
- scroll through the *Directory Tree* until you can see the branch containing the directory;
- expand the branch of the directory tree that contains your directory; or
- collapse other branches of the directory tree to make the display manageable.

SCROLLING THE DIRECTORY TREE

Figure 32. This is a scroll bar showing its various parts.

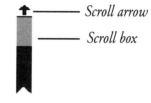

Scroll arrow

Scroll box

MOUSE

To move through the *Directory Tree* window, do one of the following:
- click on the top or bottom scroll arrow;
- drag the scroll box up or down; or
- click in the darker area of the scroll bar.

KEYBOARD

Figure 33. Press the Up Arrow or Down Arrow key until you select the directory.

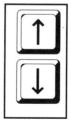

*Note: You can also use the Home, End, Page Up, or Page Down keys to move the cursor more rapidly. See **Selecting and Finding Files** from the **Working with Files** section.*

EXPANDING BRANCHES

The Shell marks directories that have undisplayed subdirectories with a "+" sign.

MOUSE

Figure 34. Click on the "+" sign of the directory and the Shell displays the next level of subdirectories.

Figure 35. Press the Tab key until you have highlighted the *Directory Tree* window title bar. Use the Up Arrow or Down Arrow key to highlight the directory at the top of the branch, then press the "+" (plus) key.

COLLAPSING BRANCHES

MOUSE

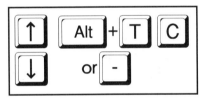

Figure 36. Click on the directory you wish to collapse. (It will have a "-" sign in it.)

KEYBOARD

Figure 37. Use the Up Arrow or Down Arrow key to move to the directory you want to collapse and call up the menu command **Tree**/*Collapse Branch* (Alt+T, followed by a C) or just press the "-" key.

EXPANDING AN ENTIRE DIRECTORY BRANCH

MOUSE

Select the directory at the top of the branch and call up the menu command, **Tree**/*Expand Branch*.

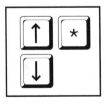

KEYBOARD

Figure 38. Select the directory at the top of the branch (Up Arrow or Down Arrow) then press the "*" key.

With either the keyboard or the mouse, this shows all of the subdirectory levels.

COLLAPSING AN ENTIRE DIRECTORY BRANCH

MOUSE

Select the directory at the top of the branch and call up the menu command **Tree**/*Collapse branch.*

KEYBOARD

Figure 39. Select the directory at the top of the branch (Up Arrow) then press the "-" key.

EXPANDING ALL DIRECTORIES ON A DRIVE

MOUSE

Call up the **Tree**/*Expand All* command.

KEYBOARD

Figure 40. Press the Ctrl+* keys.

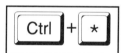

COLLAPSING ALL DIRECTORIES ON A DRIVE

MOUSE

Figure 41. Click on the root directory icon.

KEYBOARD

Figure 42. Select the root directory (Up Arrow), then call up the menu command **Tree**/*Collapse Branch* (Alt+T, followed by a C) or just press the "-" key (the keyboard shortcut).

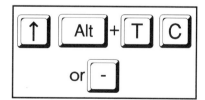

CREATING DIRECTORIES

MS-DOS automatically creates the root directory while formatting a disk. All other directories on a disk are subdirectories of the root directory.

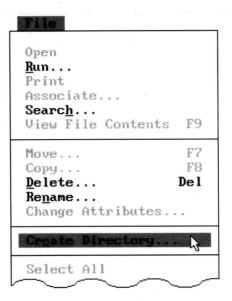

Figure 43. You can choose the File/ *Create Directory* command when you have activated the *Directory Tree* area.

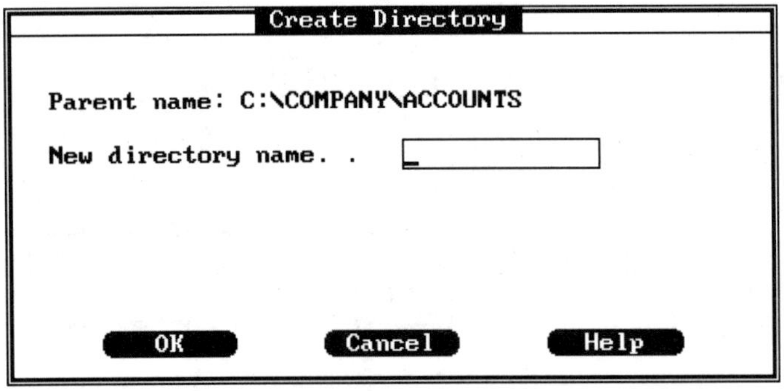

Figure 44. This command displays the *Create Directory* dialog box. Enter the name of the new directory in the *New directory name* text box. Click on *OK* to create the directory.

DELETING DIRECTORIES

Figure 45. You can use the **File**/*Delete* command after you select the *Directory Tree* area. Note that you can delete only directories that are empty, so you have to delete the files inside first.

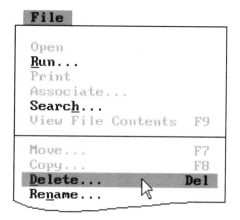

Figure 46. The *Delete Directory Confirmation* dialog box asks you before deleting a directory. Note that the option to confirm your action is on by default.

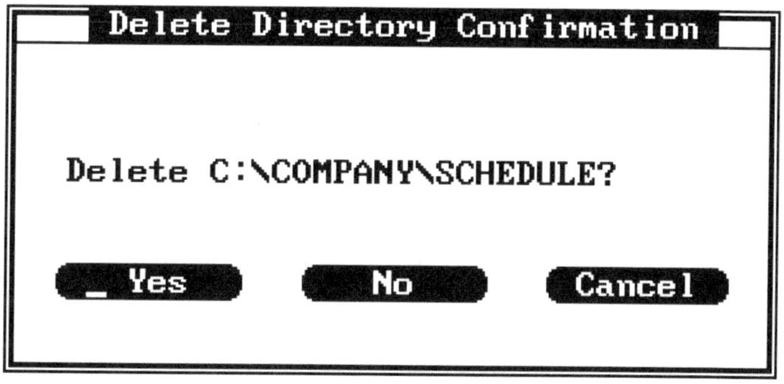

RENAMING DIRECTORIES

You can rename directories as long as there isn't anorher directory with the same name in the branch and at that level.

Figure 47. To rename a directory, select the *Directory Tree* window, choose the directory and call up the **File**/*Rename* command.

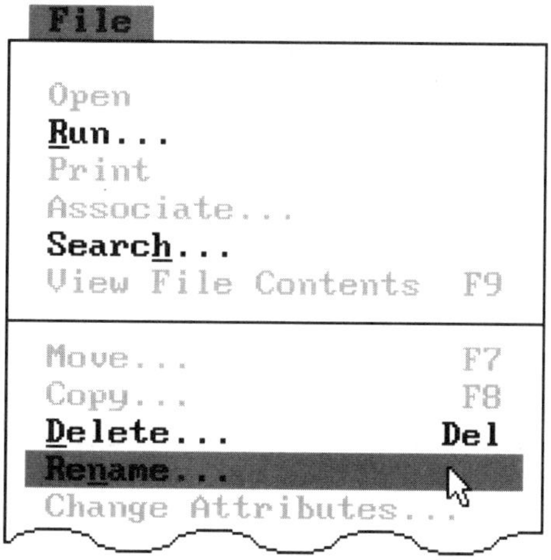

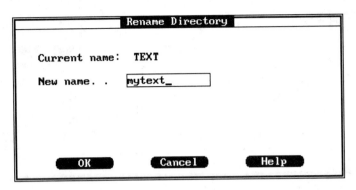

Figure 48. The *Rename* command displays the *Rename Directory* dialog box. Enter the name of the new directory into the *New name* text box of the *Rename Directory* dialog box, then select *OK*.

DIRECTORY STATISTICS

Although the *File List* displays the files in the currently selected directory, you can't tell at a glance whether or not, for example, all files will fit onto a floppy disk. The **Options**/*Show Information* command lets you see more information about files, directories, and disks.

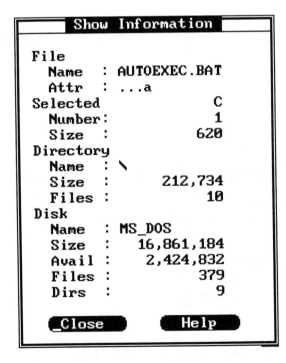

Figure 49. You can see from the *Show Information* dialog box the number of files in the selected directory and its size. The selected directory, in this example, contains 10 files with a total size of 212,734 bytes.

WORKING WITH FILES

Figure 50. The *File List* area displays the name, size, and date of the last modification of each file in the current directory. This area is the "work bench" for many file management tasks, such as selecting, finding, viewing, printing, and renaming files.

D:\PERSONAL*.*		
APPNTMNT.DOC	8,959	02-05-93
BANKLOAN.XLS	10,774	09-07-93
BBS_MAIL.MSG	639	03-06-93
DOS6VQG .TXT	5,888	03-08-93
HOWZAT .DOC	1,376	03-07-93
MONICA .LUV	1,216	08-09-93
MYTRUCK .GIF	5,223	03-08-93
SURF .WAV	9,058	02-03-93
WEBSTERS.XLS	11,165	05-06-92

SELECTING AND FINDING FILES

The Shell provides excellent facilities to find and select files.

SELECTING A SINGLE FILE

MOUSE

Figure 51. Click on a scroll arrow until you can see the file you want in the *File List* area, then click on the file.

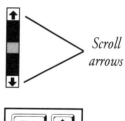

Scroll arrows

KEYBOARD

Figure 52. Press the Tab key until you have activated the *File List* area, then use the Up Arrow or Down Arrow key to move the selection cursor to the file you want. This may scroll the file list in the list area.

You can also use the following keys in the *File List* area:

Home	Selects the first file in the list.
End	Selects the last file in the list.
Page Up	Selects the first file in the previous window.
Page Down	Selects the last file in the next window.

When you have highlighted the file, press the Enter key.

You can also select a file by typing the first letter of its name. If there is more than one file beginning with the same letter, press the key again to move to the next file that starts with that letter.

SELECTING A GROUP OF ADJACENT FILES

MOUSE

Figure 53. Click on the first file in the group, hold down the Shift key and select the last file in the group. This selects all files between the first and last in the group.

KEYBOARD

Figure 54. Select the first file in the group; then hold down the Shift key and use the Up Arrow or Down Arrow key to move the selection cursor to the last file in the group. As you move the selection cursor over a file, it is added to the highlighted group.

ADDING FILES TO A FILE SELECTION

MOUSE

Figure 55. Hold down the Ctrl key and click each file you want to add to the selection. You can select non-adjacent files this way.

KEYBOARD

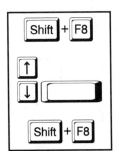

Figure 56. Press Shift+F8 to turn on *Add Mode*. The word *Add* appears in the status bar. Use the Arrow keys to move the selection cursor to the name of a file you wish to add to the current selection and press the Spacebar. Add all the files you want to in the same way, then press Shift+F8 to turn off *Add Mode*.

CLEARING A SELECTION

MOUSE

Figure 57. Click on another file without holding down either the Shift or the Ctrl key.

KEYBOARD

Figure 58. Press the Up Arrow or Down Arrow key and the Shell deselects any files you had selected.

SELECTING ALL FILES

Figure 59. The File/*Select All* command selects all files in the current directory.

Alternatively, you can press Alt+F (which selects the File menu) and then S (to select the *Select All* command).

DESELECTING ALL FILES

Figure 60. The File/*Deselect All* command deselects all files in the current selection.

The keyboard commands are Alt+F and then L (to select the *Deselect All* command).

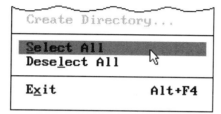

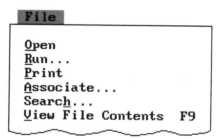

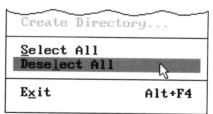

REMOVING A SINGLE FILE FROM A SELECTION OF FILES

MOUSE

Figure 61. Hold down the Ctrl key and click on the file.

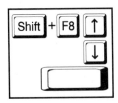

Figure 62. Press Shift+F8 to turn on *Add Mode* and then move the selection cursor over the file you want to deselect, then press the Spacebar.

INCREASING THE SIZE OF THE FILE LIST AREA

Invoke the *Single File List* command from the **View** menu.

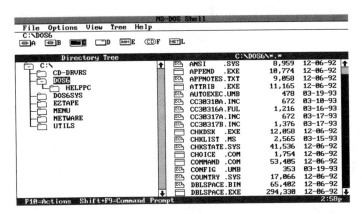

Figure 63. This figure shows the Shell screen after invoking the View/*Single File List* option.

Note the extended file list area to the right of the screen. You can return to the default Shell screen by selecting *Program/File Lists* from the **View** menu.

SELECTING FROM MULTIPLE DIRECTORIES

Figure 64. Invoke the Options/ *Select Across Directories* command to select files from different directories. The files remain selected as you change directories in the *Directory Tree* window.

You should be aware that any commands you select affect all selected files, even when you do not display them in the *File List* area.

FILE LIST OPTIONS

Figure 65. You can use the Op-tions/*File Display Options* command to control the type of files that the *File List* area lists and the order in which they appear. The *File Display Options* dialog box gives you various options, as explained below.

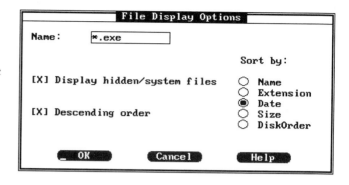

The *Name* box lets you enter file name masks or filters so you can limit the files that the file list area displays to those that you want to see.

If you want to see hidden and system files, all you have to do is check the *Display hidden/system files* check box.

The radio buttons under the *Sort by* option give you control over the files list. Choose whichever order suits you.

Descending order affects how the Shell sorts the files; in the example, the Shell will list files starting with the oldest file.

DISPLAYING ALL FILES

Figure 66. Activating the View/*All Files* command lists all files on the selected drive wherever they are. This is useful if you have set a file mask to restrict the number of files the list displays.

For example, you can view all your programs, as shown here, by choosing the View/*All Files* command after setting an **.exe* file filter (as we did in Figure 65).

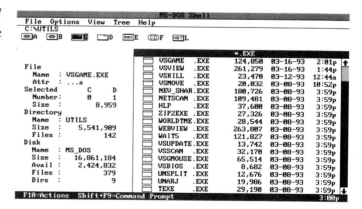

SEARCHING FOR FILES

The File/*Search* command opens the *Search File* dialog box (Figure 67). You specify the search criterion in the *Search for* text box. If necessary, set or clear the *Search entire disk* option and then click on *OK*.

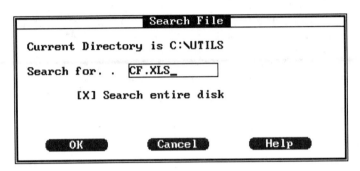

Figure 67. The *Search File* dialog box in this example shows we are looking for a cashflow analysis (CF) created in MS Excel. We have checked the *Search entire disk* checkbox, so the search extends through all directories, otherwise the Shell would search only the current directory.

VIEWING FILES

Figure 68. To view the contents of files, select the File/*View File Contents* command or press F9.

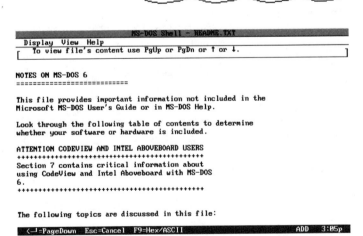

Figure 69. This figure shows the contents of a text file opened through the *View File Contents* command. You use the Page Down and Page Up keys to scroll through the text. Press the Esc key to return to the main screen.

PRINTING FILES

Figure 70. To print text files, select the *Print* command from the File menu. The keyboard equivalent is Alt+F and P.

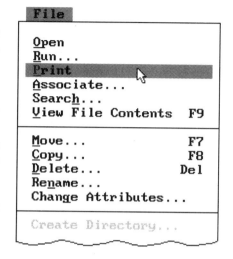

You need to load the MS-DOS Print program before starting the Shell to print files. For a discussion of the Print program, see the **Printing Files** section of Chapter 4, Command Line Survival.

To print files in the Shell, select the files you want and choose the File/*Print* command.

DELETING FILES

Figure 71. Select any files you want to delete, then choose the File/*Delete* command. When you select a group of files, the *Delete File* dialog box asks if you want to delete the files. You can use the Left and Right Arrow keys to scroll through the selected files listed in the *Delete* text box. Select *Cancel* if you want to keep the files or *OK* to delete them.

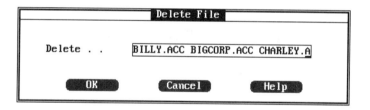

Figure 72. The *Delete File Confirmation* dialog box asks you whether you want to delete each selected file.

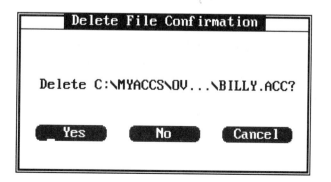

If you select a single file to delete, the *No* and *Cancel* buttons have the same effect. The effect of these buttons is different if the Shell is, say, deleting the third of five files. Selecting *No* saves this file and the Shell begins processing the rest of the selection. Selecting *Cancel* aborts the command; the Shell does not process the remaining files.

MISCELLANEOUS FILE OPERATIONS

RENAMING FILES

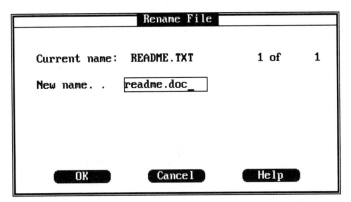

Figure 73. To rename selected files, choose the File/*Rename* command. The *Rename File* dialog box appears for each file you selected, showing the name of the file and the order in which it appears in the overall selection.

You key the new name of the file into the *New name* text box and click on *OK*.

SAFEGUARDING FILES

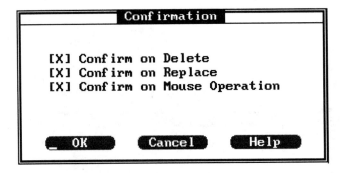

Figure 74. Select the Options/ *Confirmation* command to call up the *Confirmation* dialog box.

Confirm on Delete verifies whether you want to delete a file. *Confirm on Replace* verifies whether you want to replace an existing file. *Confirm on Mouse Operation* verifies whether you want to complete mouse-based actions such as moving and copying files.

CHANGING FILE ATTRIBUTES

Figure 75. File attributes are switches that influence a file. You can set (turn on) or clear (turn off) each switch and work with combinations of these attributes. This table describes the attributes you can assign to files.

To change the attributes of a file, select it and choose the **File/** *Change Attributes* command. From the *Change Attributes* dialog box, set the attributes you want and click on *OK*.

System	Used for important MS-DOS operating system files. You cannot delete, copy, or replace files with this attribute.
Hidden	Provides the same level of protection as the system attribute, but does not designate it as a system file.
Archive	Used by the backup, restore, and xcopy commands. The attribute indicates you have updated the file since you last backed it up.
Read Only	Prevents you from deleting, moving, replacing, or updating a file. You can only copy or read a file with this attribute.

Figure 76. The *Change Attributes* dialog box shows the four file attributes that you can set or clear: *Hidden, System, Archive*, or *Read-only*.

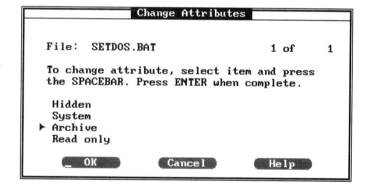

TRANSFERRING FILES WITH THE MOUSE

Figure 77. To move the selected source files from the directory *overdue* to the destination directory *aged*, you first place the mouse pointer in the file selection and hold the left mouse button down.

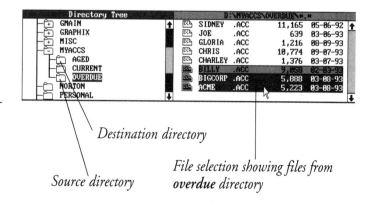

Destination directory

Source directory

File selection showing files from ***overdue*** *directory*

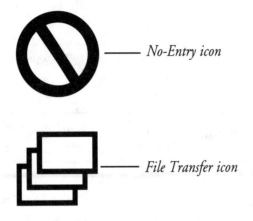

No-Entry icon

Figure 78. As soon as you move the mouse, the mouse pointer appears as a No-Entry icon. Releasing the mouse button at this stage cancels the operation.

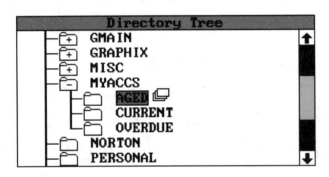

File Transfer icon

Figure 79. As you move the mouse cursor into the *Directory Tree* window, it appears as the File Transfer icon.

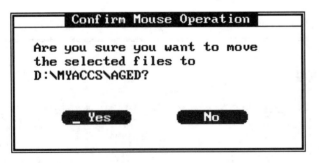

Figure 80. Release the left mouse button when you have highlighted the destination directory you want (in this case *aged*).

Figure 81. If you have not changed the default setting for the *Confirm on Mouse Operation* option (see Figure 74), the Shell displays the *Confirm Mouse Operation* dialog box. You can cancel the operation by clicking on *No* if you have made an error.

Figure 82. If you have not changed the default setting for the *Confirm on Replace* option, and copying the file would replace a file in the destination directory, the Shell displays the *Replace File Confirmation* dialog box. Select the *Cancel* button if you don't want to replace the file. The Shell then processes the remaining files in the group.

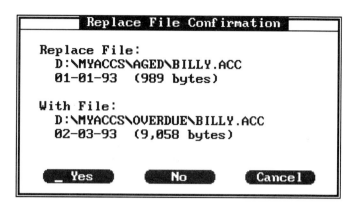

Points to remember when dragging files:

• The No-Entry icon appears when you try to drag files into an area where you can't put them. You can release the mouse button to cancel the operation.

• Drag files to a drive icon to *copy* them into the root directory of that drive.

• When you drag files between directories, you are *moving* the files to the destination directory. You can *copy* the file to the directory by holding down the Control key.

• If the destination directory is on another drive, you need to display both the source and directory trees at once. Select the *Dual File Lists* command from the **View** menu to see two separate directories or drives simultaneously.

TRANSFERRING FILES WITH THE KEYBOARD

You can also copy or move files with the **File**/*Copy* and **File**/ *Move* commands. The advantage of these commands is that you can rename the files in the process.

Figure 83. Select those files you want to copy or move and choose the **File**/*Move* or **File**/*Copy* command. (You can also press F7 to move and F8 to copy.) The Shell opens the *Move File* or *Copy File* dialog box; enter the destination directory in the *To* text box.

If you enter only the directory name, the Shell copies each file to that directory with the file's existing name. You can specify a new name by including the file name. Click on *OK* to accept the command or you can cancel the operation by clicking on *No.* If necessary, respond to the *Replace File Confirmation* dialog box.

WORKING WITH PROGRAMS

The Shell provides two ways of running programs. The first lets you run a program that is in the *File List* area. The second permits you to run a program without displaying it in the *File List* area. If you double-click on the program name or icon in the *File List* box, this runs the program.

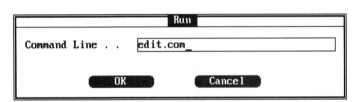

Figure 84. For a program that you haven't displayed in the *File List* area, select the File/*Run* command and the Shell opens the *Run* dialog box. Enter the name of the program in the *Command Line* text box and click on *OK.*

ASSOCIATING FILES

You can *associate* files with the applications you use to generate these files. For example, you can tell the Shell that a certain word processor has produced a certain document even though it hasn't. Once you have done this, you can double-click the document's icon and the word processor opens the document. This linking is called "associating."

ASSOCIATING A FILE WITH A PROGRAM

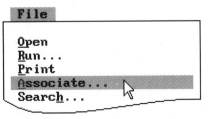

Figure 85. The File/*Associate* command associates applications with document files they produce. This command opens the *Associate File* dialog box (Figure 86).

Figure 86. In this example, the association is between Excel and files with the extension *xls*.

Another way you can associate a file with a program is to select the file and enter the program that you want it associated with. You can do this in another *Associate File* dialog box (Figure 87).

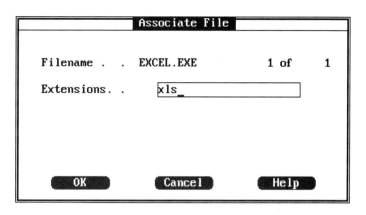

REMOVING AN ASSOCIATION

Figure 87. Select the file in the *File List* window you want to dissociate and then choose the **File/ Associate** command. In the dialog box, press the Backspace key to delete the program name, then click on *OK*.

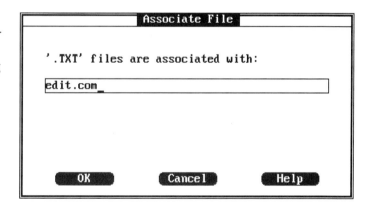

OPENING AN ASSOCIATED FILE

MOUSE

Figure 88. Double-click on the file name or icon.

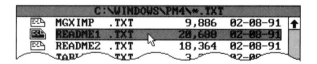

KEYBOARD

Figure 89. Select the file, then the **File/ *Open*** command; alternatively, select the file and press Enter.

 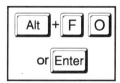

PROGRAM LIST

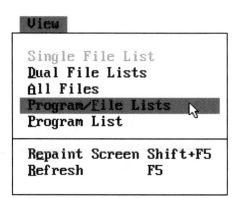

Figure 90. The View/*Program/File Lists* command activates the *Program* and *File* list boxes. The *Program List* command activates the program list only.

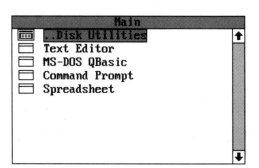

Figure 91. The *Program List* area, which appears by default, shows the Main program group. As you can see in this figure, it contains programs and program groups.

Program group

Program

Figure 92. Icons containing program icons represent program groups. Empty icons represent programs (applications). For example, the Text Editor is the program *edit.com* and Spreadsheet refers to *excel.exe*.

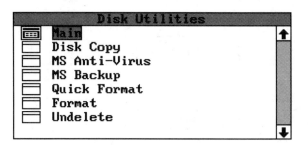

Figure 93. The *Disk Utilities* group contains important file and disk maintenance programs. Selecting the Main group icon re-displays the Main group shown in Figure 91 (above).

RUNNING A PROGRAM

MOUSE

Figure 94. Double-click on the program's icon.

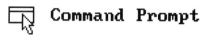

KEYBOARD

Figure 95. Press Tab until the *Program List* area is selected. Use the Arrow keys to move the selection cursor over the program name, then press the Enter key.

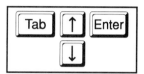

MAINTAINING THE PROGRAM LIST

Figure 96. When you work with the *Program List*, the commands in the **File** menu change.

Figure 97. This table shows what each command in the *Program List* **File** menu does.

New	Adds a new program or program group to the Program List.
Open	Runs a selected program or opens a selected program group.
Copy	Copies programs from one group to another.
Delete	Deletes a selected program or program group.
Properties	Updates the details of an item in the Program List.
Reorder	Changes the order in which you list items in the Program List.
Run	Executes the program.
Exit	Exits the MS-DOS Shell.

ADDING A PROGRAM ITEM TO A PROGRAM GROUP

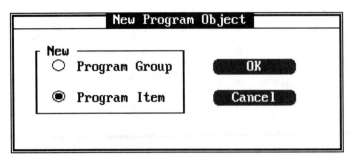

Figure 98. To add a new item to a program group, select the group where you wish to add the program and choose the File/*New* command, which opens the *New Program Object* dialog box.

Choose the *Program Item* radio button and select *OK*.

Figure 99. The Shell then opens the *Add Program* dialog box.

In the *Program Title* text box, type in what you want the list to show for the program, then add the program's full pathname in the *Commands* text box.

In this example, entering the "%1" parameter tells the Shell to prompt you to enter a file name whenever you choose to run Excel. You can enter a *Startup Directory*, which normally contains your program's data files.

You can give the application a *Shortcut Key* combination. The Shell doesn't let you use combinations that conflict with shortcuts you have given other programs. Select the *Application Shortcut Key* text box and press F1 to see a list of those shortcuts that you can't use.

Turn *Pause after exit* on if you want a pause as you exit the program. This is useful if you need a pause before returning to the Shell; for example if you want to see any messages the program creates when you exit. When you are ready to return to the Shell, you can press any key.

You can password-protect the program to ensure that only people who know the password can run it. If you want to do this, type the password into the *Password* text box (it can be up to 20 characters, including spaces), then click on *OK*. The Shell asks for the password each time you run the program.

ADDING A NEW PROGRAM GROUP

Figure 100. Open the program group where you want to add the new group, and call up the File/ *New* command.

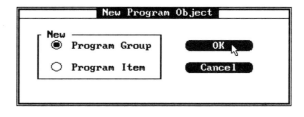

In the *New Program Object* dialog box that appears, choose the *Program Group* radio button and click on *OK*. The Shell then opens the *Add Group* dialog box.

Figure 101. In this figure, we are creating a new program group called *games* in the *Add Group* dialog box.

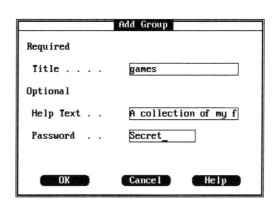

You can enter *Help Text* for the group giving, for example, a description of the programs that are in the group. The Shell displays the *Help Text* when you select the group and press the F1 key.

You can password-protect the group by entering a password into the *Password* text box.

COPYING A PROGRAM ITEM

Figure 102. Select the program item you want to copy and choose the File/ *Copy* command. The status bar displays the message: *Display the group to copy to, then Press F2*. Open the group where you want to copy the item, then press the F2 key.

`Display the group to copy to, then press F2.`

UPDATING A PROGRAM ITEM OR GROUP

```
┌──────────── Program Item Properties ────────────┐
│                                                  │
│  Program Title . . . .  Editor_                  │
│                                                  │
│  Commands  . . . . . .  EDIT %1                  │
│                                                  │
│  Startup Directory . .  [                    ]   │
│                                                  │
│  Application Shortcut Key  [                 ]   │
│                                                  │
│  [ ] Pause after exit    Password . .  [      ]  │
│                                                  │
│     ( OK )    ( Cancel )    ( Help )  ( Advanced...) │
└──────────────────────────────────────────────────┘
```

Figure 103. If you need to change the title of a program or group, or alter the command to run a program, you have to alter the item or group properties.

Select the program item or group and then the **File**/*Properties* command. The Shell displays the *Program Item Properties* or *Program Group Properties* dialog box, which is similar to the *Add Program* (Figure 99) or the *Add Group* (Figure 101) dialog box. Once you have edited the details, click *OK*.

DELETING A PROGRAM ITEM OR GROUP

```
┌──────────────── Delete Item ────────────────┐
│                                              │
│  1. Delete this item.                        │
│  2. Do not delete this item.                 │
│                                              │
│    ( OK )        ( Cancel )       ( Help )   │
└──────────────────────────────────────────────┘
```

Figure 104. Select the program item or group and choose the **File**/*Delete* command or press the Del key. The Shell opens the *Delete Item* dialog box, where you highlight the action you want and click on *OK*.

When deleting a group, first delete all programs and program groups belonging to that group.

REORDERING THE ITEMS IN A PROGRAM GROUP

```
Select location to move to, then press ENTER.
```

Figure 105. Open the group you want to reorder. Select the first thing you want to move and choose the **File**/*Reorder* command. The message *Select location to move to, then press Enter* appears in the status bar.

Double-click on the new location, or move the selection cursor to this new location and press the Enter key. Repeat these steps for any other objects that you need to relocate.

TASK SWAPPER

The *Task Swapper* allows you to work on several tasks at the one time, swapping between them at will.

Figure 106. The *Active Task List* shows the active applications. *Task Swapper* allows you to swap between tasks without terminating them, which saves time and reduces loss of continuity.

However, it takes up a fair amount of computer memory so you should disable the *Task Swapper* when you don't need it.

USING THE TASK SWAPPER

Figure 107. To use the *Task Swapper*, select the **Options**/*Enable Task Swapper* command. The dot beside *Enable Task Swapper* shows that you have enabled it. You disable the *Task Swapper* by selecting it again.

RUNNING SEVERAL PROGRAMS SIMULTANEOUSLY

You can use any method we described to run a program. If the program is in the *Program List*, the *Task Swapper* displays its title in the *Active Task List*, otherwise it displays the program's file name.

RETURNING FROM A PROGRAM TO THE SHELL

Press the Ctrl+Esc key combination. You will see the Shell screen as it was before you started the program.

RETURNING TO A PROGRAM FROM THE SHELL

MOUSE

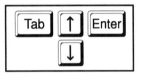

Figure 108. Double-click the icon representing the program in the *Active Task List*.

KEYBOARD

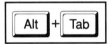

Figure 109. Press Tab until you have highlighted the *Active Task List* window. Press Up Arrow or Down Arrow until you have selected the icon representing the program. Then choose the **File**/*Open* command or simply press Enter.

SWAPPING FROM ONE PROGRAM TO ANOTHER

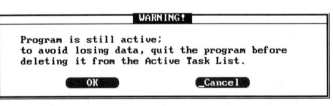

Figure 110. Hold down the Alt key and press the Tab key until you display the title of the program you want at the top of the screen, then release the Alt key.

TERMINATING AN ACTIVE PROGRAM

```
┌──────────────── WARNING! ────────────────┐
│                                           │
│  Program is still active;                 │
│  to avoid losing data, quit the program before │
│  deleting it from the Active Task List.   │
│                                           │
│       OK                  Cancel          │
│                                           │
└───────────────────────────────────────────┘
```

Figure 111. Select the program from the *Active Task List* and choose *Delete* from the **File** menu. Select *OK* from the *Warning* dialog box, or select *Cancel* to switch to the program you want to close and exit from it.

MS-DOS EDITOR

6

INTRODUCTION

The Editor is a quick, simple-to-use program that is well suited for memos, notes, lists, and batch program files. (For more about batch programs, see **Chapter 8, Advanced Command Techniques.**)

The Editor uses menus, dialog boxes, list boxes, and other elements found in many word processing packages. You access these with the mouse or the keyboard.

STARTING THE EDITOR

Figure 1. Type "edit" on the command line to start the Editor.

This activates *edit.com* in the DOS directory to run the Editor. *Edit.com* relies on *QBasic.exe* and *edit.hlp*. Keep these files in the DOS directory.

Figure 2. You can add the path name of a file to the *Edit* command. The command shown in this figure starts the Editor and then loads *myfile.txt* ready for you to edit.

Figure 3. Alternatively, you can start the Editor in the MS-DOS Shell. To do this, double-click on Editor in the Main group.

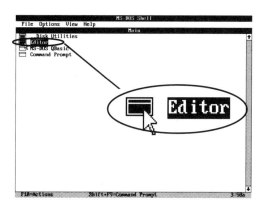

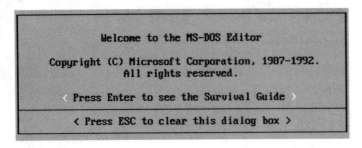

```
         Welcome to the MS-DOS Editor

  Copyright (C) Microsoft Corporation, 1987-1992.
              All rights reserved.

  < Press Enter to see the Survival Guide >

  < Press ESC to clear this dialog box >
```

Figure 4. When you start the Editor without a path name command, MS-DOS displays a copyright notice.

Press Enter to view the *Survival Guide*, which is an on-line help facility that tells you how to use the Editor. For example, you can use it to see what particular keys do what.

Text cursor   *Menu bar*   *Filename*

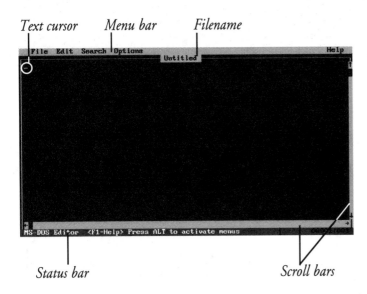

Status bar   *Scroll bars*

Figure 5. To use the Editor, press Esc or click on the line *Press Esc to clear this dialog box.* The Editor text entry screen appears; this figure highlights the main parts of the screen.

The menu bar lets you perform various tasks in the Editor. This chapter explains the menu commands in detail.

The Editor displays the name of the current file just below the menu bar.

The cursor is an underscore that blinks in the top left corner of the screen, below the menu bar. As you type, text appears on the screen at the cursor position.

The scroll bars enable you to move through the document with the mouse.

The status bar displays a variety of messages.

ENTERING TEXT

Figure 6. As you type, the Editor displays characters on the screen, but unlike word processors, the Editor doesn't automatically wrap text from line to line. You have to press Enter to start a new line.

Figure 7. This table shows you some keys you use frequently when entering and editing text in the Editor.

Key	Function
Enter	Starts a new line. Lines can be up to 256 characters.
Backspace	Deletes the last character typed.
Del	Deletes the character at the cursor.
Ctrl+T	Deletes a word if the cursor is on the first letter of a word.
Ins	Changes between *Insert* and *Overtype* modes.

ENTRY MODES

Figure 8. The Editor has two entry modes: *Insert* and *Overtype*.

In Insert mode, the cursor appears as an underscore. With this mode, the Editor inserts the text you type at the cursor position. The cursor pushes any text to its right along the line to make room for the new text.

Figure 9. In Overtype mode, the cursor appears as a small square. As you type, you replace any text that is under the cursor.

You swap between these modes by pressing the Insert key.

MOVING THE TEXT CURSOR

Key	Moves the cursor
Arrow keys	One character (left or right) or one line (up or down).
Home	To the beginning of the line.
End	To the end of the line.
Ctrl+Home	To the beginning of the file.
Ctrl+End	To the end of the file.

Figure 10. This table shows you which keys you can use to move your cursor around. Clicking on the new location with the mouse also moves the cursor.

INSERTING BLANK LINES

Figure 11. Use the Home key to move to the beginning of the line, then press Enter to add a blank line between existing lines.

FILE MENU

The **File** menu contains commands to create, open, save, and print files.

NEW COMMAND

Figure 12. Click on the *New* command in the **File** menu to create a new file.

Alternatively, you can press Alt+F to drop the **File** menu and then press the highlighted letter for *New* (N).

Figure 13. If you have a file open when you select *New*, the Editor closes that file and asks whether you want to save any changes.

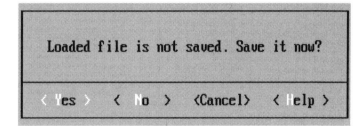

Click on *Yes* to save the document, close it, and open a new file. Click on *No* to open a new file and to close the current document without saving the changes. *Cancel* abandons the operation. Alternatively, you can press the highlighted keys. Pressing the Esc key is equivalent to clicking on *Cancel*.

Figure 14. The Editor temporarily names the new file as *Untitled*.

OPEN COMMAND

To open an existing file, select *Open* from the **File** menu.

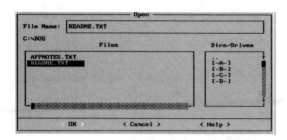

Figure 15. The *Open* dialog box appears on the screen. Type "*.txt" into the *File Name* text box and the *Files* list box shows all files with a *.txt* extension. You can change the text in the *File Name* text box to show any files you need to access.

Double-clicking on an option in the *Dirs/Drives* list box changes the current drive or directory.

If you do not have a mouse, use the following keys to move around dialog boxes:

• Tab key moves between fields.
• Arrow keys select items within fields.
• Enter key executes.
• Esc cancels.

You double-click on the file name to open a file; or press the Tab key until the cursor is in the *Files* list box, then with the Up or Down Arrow key select your file and press Enter. The Editor displays the file on screen in both cases.

SAVE COMMAND

The *Save* command in the **File** menu saves files instantly. It simply updates the existing file with any changes you have made.

Current directory —

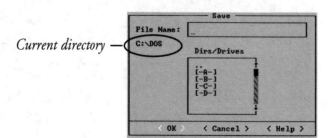

Figure 16. If you choose *Save* from the **File** menu and you haven't previously saved the file, the Editor displays the *Save* dialog box.

Double-clicking on an option in the *Dirs/Drives* list box chooses the file location (i.e. a directory). The dialog box displays the current directory under the *File Name* text box.

If you want to use the keyboard, Tab to the *Dirs/Drives* list, select the directory you want with the Up or Down Arrow key, and then press Enter.

Figure 17. With the cursor in the *File Name* text box, type in the name of the file. You need to add an extension because the Editor doesn't do this automatically.

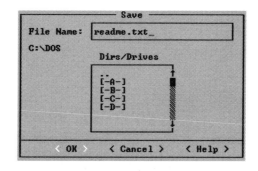

Figure 18. Clicking on *OK* or pressing Enter saves the file and returns you to the editing screen. The Editor now displays your filename at the top of the screen.

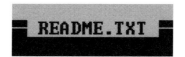

SAVE AS COMMAND

The *Save As* command saves a file under a new name. For example, if you are creating slightly different text files, save the first file, make the necessary changes, and then save it under a different name.

Figure 19. The *Save As* dialog box works the same way as the *Save* dialog box. Initially, choose where you want to put the file from the *Dirs/Drives* list box, then type the name of the file into the *File Name* text box.

Clicking on *OK* (or pressing Enter) saves the file and returns you to the Edit screen.

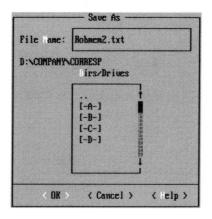

PRINT COMMAND

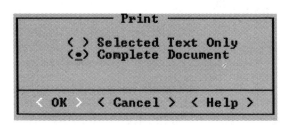

Figure 20. When you select the *Print* command in the **File** menu, it activates the *Print* dialog box. The *Print* dialog box gives you two options—printing only the text you have selected, or a complete file. Simply click on the option you want or press the Tab key to switch between them.

To start printing, click on *OK*.

EXIT COMMAND

To exit from the Editor, select *Exit* from the **File** menu or press Alt+F then X.

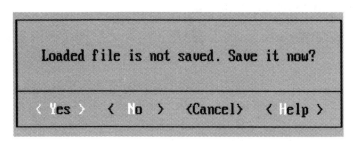

Figure 21. If you have made changes to a document that you have not saved and you attempt to exit, the Editor asks you if you want to save the file.

To save it and close the Editor, click on *Yes*. Clicking on *No* closes the Editor but doesn't save the changes in the file you have open. *Cancel* abandons the operation and leaves you in the Editor.

EDIT MENU

The **Edit** menu contains commands to copy, move, or delete selected text. When you cut or copy a block of text, you can paste it anywhere in your document as many times as you like.

SELECTING TEXT

Figure 22. You need to select (highlight) text before you can use the options in the **Edit** menu. In this case, the Editor displays selected text as dark text on a light background.

You can select text with the mouse or the keyboard.

Selected text

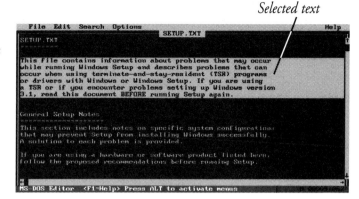

SELECTING TEXT WITH THE MOUSE

To select text with the mouse, put the cursor at the beginning of the text you want to select, then hold down the left mouse button and drag over the text you want to select.

Dragging the cursor horizontally selects text on the one line. Dragging vertically selects whole lines of text. Release the mouse button when you have selected all the text you need.

SELECTING TEXT WITH THE KEYBOARD

To select text with the keyboard, hold down the Shift key while moving the cursor with the Arrow keys over the text.

CUT COMMAND

Figure 23. You can use the *Cut* command to move selected text within a document and between documents. Once you have selected the text, choose *Cut* from the **Edit** menu or press Shift+Del.

The Editor removes the selected text from the screen. It stores the text in a buffer in the computer's memory called the Clipboard.

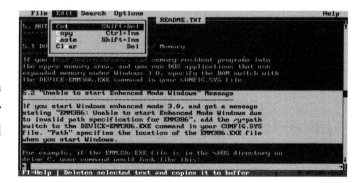

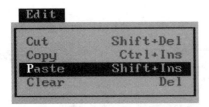

Figure 24. Put the cursor where you want to insert the text. Choose *Paste* from the **Edit** Menu or press Shift+Ins. *Paste* inserts the last text you cut into your file. You can paste the same text from the Clipboard as many times as you like.

COPY COMMAND

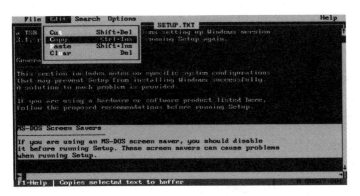

Figure 25. To copy text, select the text you wish to copy and choose *Copy* from the **Edit** menu, or press Ctrl+Ins. The Editor leaves the selected text on screen and sends a copy of the text to the Clipboard.

Figure 26. Move the insertion point to where you want to paste a copy of the text. Choosing *Paste* from the **Edit** menu inserts a copy of the text on the Clipboard into your file.

The Editor pastes the copied text at the insertion point

CLEAR COMMAND

The *Clear* command deletes text from the file and does not place the text into the Clipboard buffer. Therefore, you cannot use the *Paste* command to re-paste it into the document.

Figure 27. To clear text from the screen, select it and choose *Clear* from the **Edit** menu or press the Delete key. The Editor completely removes the text from the file.

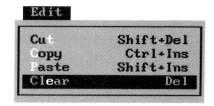

SEARCH MENU

Figure 28. The commands in the Search menu let you find specific text and make changes to it.

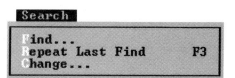

FIND COMMAND

Figure 29. The *Find* command activates the *Find* dialog box. If you want to find text, such as a particular word or name, enter the text you wish to find in the *Find What* text box.

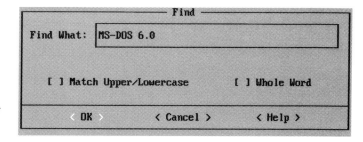

Check the *Match Upper/Lowercase* option to match exactly the case of the text in the *Find What* box. The *Whole Word* option searches for the whole word by itself, not as part of another word. For example, if you typed "the," the Editor's search would not find "the" in "mother" or any other words that contain the word "the."

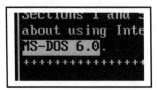

Figure 30. Selecting *OK* starts the search. The Editor highlights the first match it finds.

If you want to find the next occurrence of the word, choose the *Repeat Last Find* command in the **Search** menu.

CHANGE COMMAND

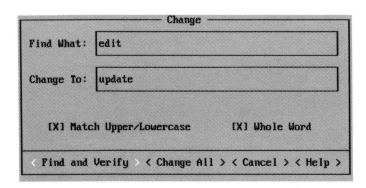

Figure 31. *Change* lets you search for specific words in a file and then replace them with something different.

For example, imagine that you wanted to replace "edit" with "update" throughout your document. Choose *Change* from the **File** menu and, in the *Change* dialog box, type "edit" into the *Find What* text box and "update" in the *Change To* text box.

Check the *Match Upper/Lowercase* option so the Editor finds *edit* in lowercase only. Check the *Whole Word* option as a precaution. This ensures that the Editor does not change "editor" to "updateor."

Figure 32. If you want to verify each change before the Editor does it, select the *Find and Verify* option in the *Change* dialog box (Figure 31). The *Change All* option in the same figure changes every occurrence of the text without asking you to confirm each change.

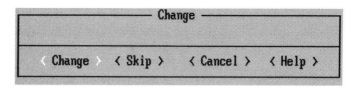

If you select the *Find and Verify* option, the Editor asks you what you want to do every time it finds a match. You can *Change* the occurrence, *Skip* over it, or *Cancel* the command.

OPTIONS MENU

Figure 33. With the **Options** menu, you can customize the Editor and set a path to the help file, *edit.hlp*.

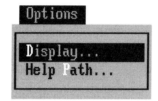

DISPLAY COMMAND

Figure 34. If you select *Display* from the **Options** menu you get the *Display* dialog box. Choose what you want as the *Foreground* and *Background* colors from the list boxes.

The sample window shows you how your selected settings look on the screen.

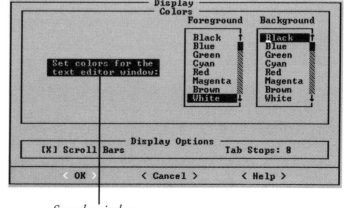

Sample window

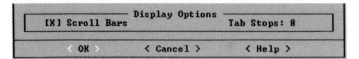

Figure 35. The Editor displays scroll bars by default. If you do not want these, de-select the *Scroll Bars* option.

You can specify the number of spaces the Editor inserts when you press the Tab key by changing the value after *Tab Stops*. The default setting is eight.

HELP PATH COMMAND

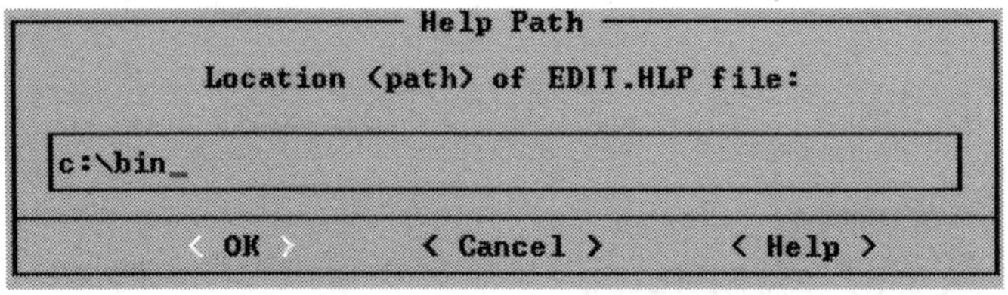

Figure 36. The *Help Path* command in the **Options** menu displays the *Help Path* dialog box. This lets you show the Editor where the *edit.hlp* file is, which contains on-line help information.

You need to specify the path only if *edit.hlp* is not in the DOS directory. To change the path, enter the directory path of *edit.hlp* into the *Location (path) of edit.hlp file* text box and click on *OK*.

In Charge of your System

7

Introduction

The innovation of MS-DOS 6 lies in the variety of tools it provides to help you manage your computer system and protect your data.

Anti-Virus

A computer virus is simply a program designed to be destructive or annoying and is often intentionally hidden from a user.

You can use simple preventative measures such as strict data management procedures to protect your computer system from a virus. However, MS-DOS 6 provides additional protection by including a virus monitoring program.

Figure 1. A computer "virus," though the name might suggest it, cannot transmit itself by its own will from one computer system to another.

Figure 2. Commonly, a virus program will infect a computer system through a network or through floppy disk distribution of programs or data.

Figure 3. Microsoft Anti-Virus detects and removes virus programs that might have already infected your computer system. Type "msav" on the command line to start Microsoft Anti-Virus.

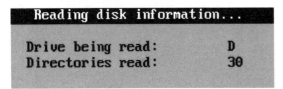

Figure 4. Microsoft Anti-Virus reads directory and file information on the current disk drive.

Menu buttons

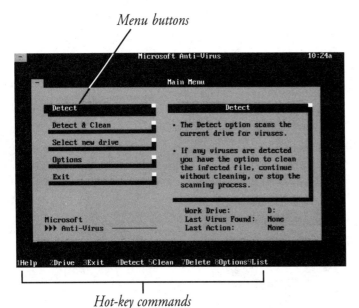

Hot-key commands

Figure 5. You use the mouse, if you have one installed, or the cursor movement keys to select the menu option you want.

The bottom line of the screen lists equivalent hot-keys for each menu button; the hot-keys use the function keys F1 to F9 on your keyboard.

Figure 6. Select the *Detect* button, or the *Detect & Clean* button if you want to remove viruses automatically. Microsoft Anti-Virus first scans your computer's memory (RAM) for virus programs.

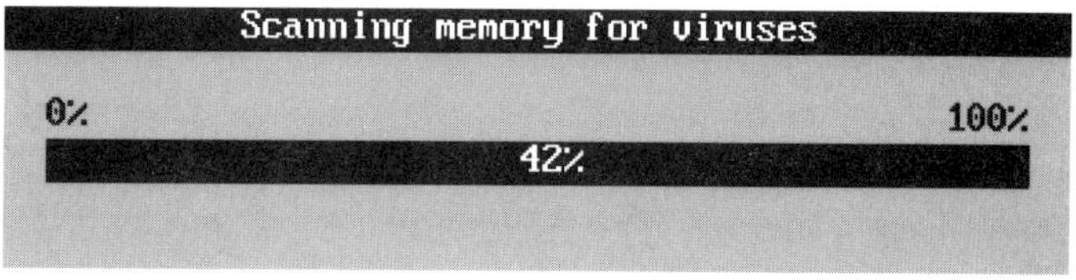

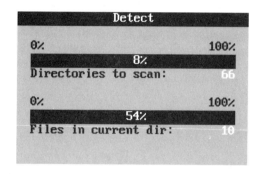

Figure 7. MS Anti-Virus then scans all the files in all directories on the current disk drive.

Figure 8. The program prompts you if it finds a virus on your computer system.

If you select the *Detect & Clean* command, MS Anti-Virus removes viruses from your computer system automatically without prompting you with virus details.

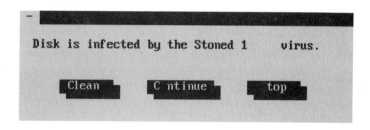

Figure 9. Once it has completed scanning for viruses, the Anti-Virus program shows you details of the detect and clean process.

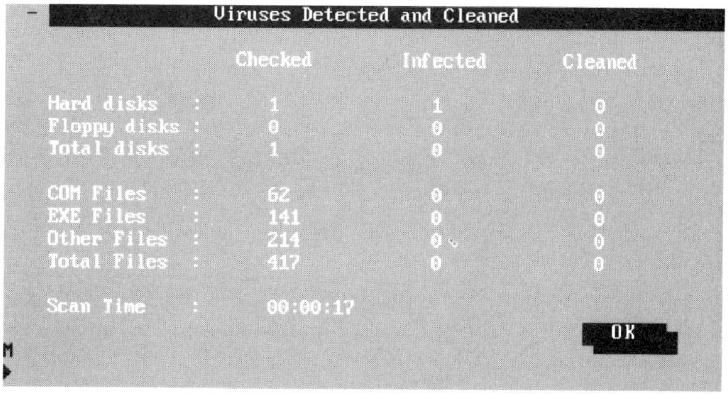

Available drive letters

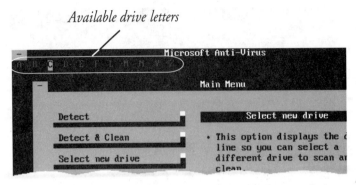

Figure 10. To scan a different drive, choose the *Select new drive* button.

MS Anti-Virus shows the available drive letters in the top left corner of the screen. Use the Left or Right Arrow key to select the drive you want and press the Enter key.

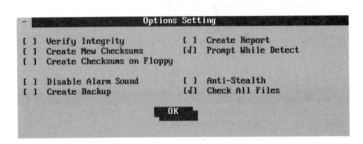

Figure 11. To configure MS Anti-Virus, select the *Options* button to bring up the *Options Setting* dialog box.

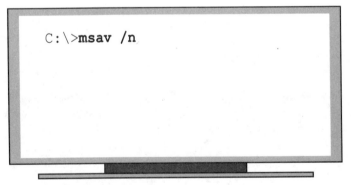

Figure 12. If you want to run MS Anti-Virus automatically without the graphical interface, start the program with the */n* option.

BACKUP

Archived files are copies of files taken from your computer system and stored independently on a removable medium such as floppy diskette or magnetic tape. You can easily retrieve archived files when you need them. Microsoft Backup provides you with an easy-to-use tool for backups.

Figure 13. Type "msbackup" on the command line to start Microsoft Backup.

Figure 14. If this is the first time you have started the program, MS Backup guides you through a number of configuration procedures, including a compatibility test. MS Backup then shows the main menu screen.

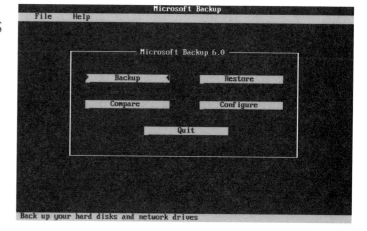

BACKING UP

SELECTING FILES TO BACK UP

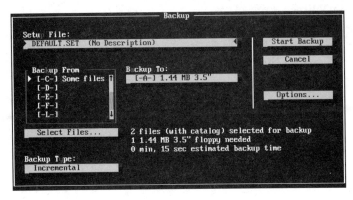

Figure 15. Choose the *Backup* button from the main menu to open the *Backup* dialog box. Select a drive in the *Backup From* box if you want a full backup of a particular drive. Select each additional drive you want to back up.

Alternatively, if you want to back up selected directories or files, choose the *Select Files* button to open the *Select Backup Files* dialog box.

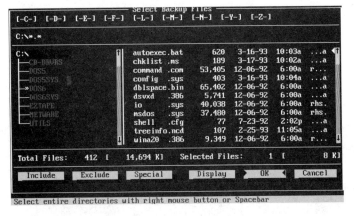

Figure 16. Choose the drive you want to back up from the list at the top of the *Select Backup Files* dialog box, then select the directory from the directory tree. *Backup* displays the file list for the directory you select. Press the Spacebar to select the entire directory from the directory tree or select files from the file list individually.

Choose the *OK* button to accept your selections and return to the screen shown in Figure 15.

SELECTING THE BACK UP TYPE

Choose the *Backup Type* button from the *Backup* screen (see Figure 15) to display the *Backup Type* dialog box shown in Figure 17. Backup gives you three ways to back up your files:

• *Full Backup*:
> Backs up all selected files.

• *Incremental Backup*:
> Backs up new and any files that have changed since the last full or incremental backup. You need a new backup set for each incremental backup.

• *Differential Backup*:
> Backs up files that have changed since the last full backup. Maintains the last differential backup set as the latest version.

Figure 17. If this is your first back-up, then select *Full* backup from the *Backup Type* dialog box, and choose the *OK* button to return to the *Backup* screen shown in Figure 15. Choose the *Start Backup* button from the *Backup* screen (see Figure 15) to begin the back-up.

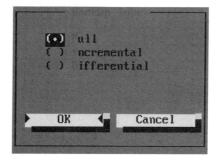

Figure 18. MS Backup shows you its progress as it backs up your selected directories and files.

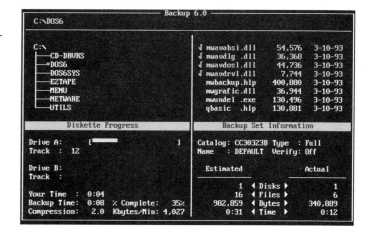

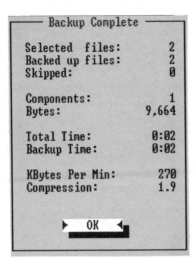

Figure 19. When it is finished, MS Backup provides statistics of the backup process.

VERIFYING YOUR BACKUP

Verifying data is very important when you back up. The *Compare* command checks that your data has not been corrupted and that your backup set matches the original files you selected to back up. The *Compare* procedure ensures you have a reliable copy of your archived files.

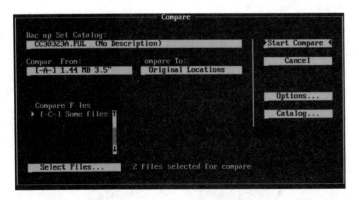

Figure 20. Choose the *Compare* button from the main menu. In the *Compare* dialog box, you can select the files you want to compare with the backup set. Choose the *Start Compare* button to begin the comparison.

RESTORING THE BACKUP SET

Figure 21. From the main menu, choose the *Catalog* button to select which backup set you want to restore.

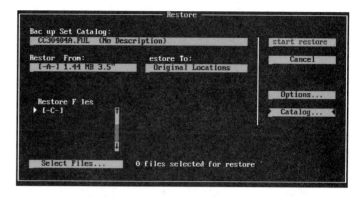

Figure 22. The *Select Catalog* dialog box lists catalog information files on your hard drive. The most fail-safe method of restoring data is to retrieve the catalog information from the backup data. Choose the *Retrieve* button from the *Select Catalog* dialog box.

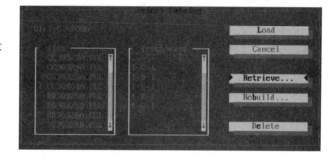

Figure 23. Select the drive on which you backed up the data. Choose the *OK* button in the *Retrieve Catalog* dialog box.

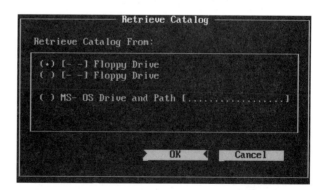

Figure 24. Backup asks you to insert the last backup disk from the set you would like to restore. This is where Backup stores catalog information. It then loads the catalog information automatically.

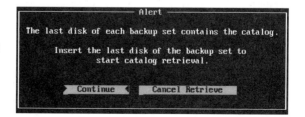

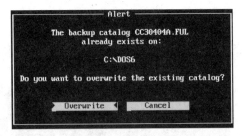

Figure 25. If you receive a warning that the catalog file exists on the hard disk, choose the *Overwrite* button to copy over it.

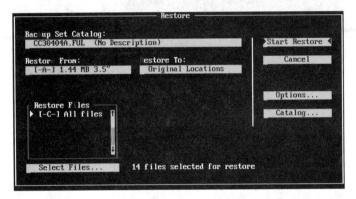

Figure 26. Once Backup loads the catalog file, it displays the *Restore* screen. You can choose the *Select Files* button to restore some of the files, or select the drive from the *Restore Files* box to restore all the files.

Once you have selected the files you want, choose the *Start Restore* button to restore them.

BACKUP OPTIONS

Select the *Options* button from the *Restore* screen (see Figure 26) to set your restore preferences.

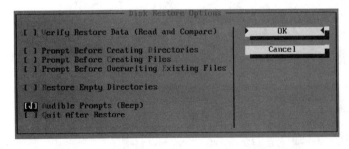

Figure 27. The *Restore Options* dialog box lets you select how Backup operates when restoring.

If you select the *Verify Restore Data* option, Backup compares each file as it backs up. This forces the backup process to slow down considerably but ensures that the backup information is secure.

The *Prompt Before...* options force Backup to check with you as it creates new files or directories before it overwrites files during a restore.

The *Restore Empty Directories* option makes sure that Backup recreates all directories during a restore, even those that contain no files.

DEFRAGMENTING DATA

MS-DOS makes the best use of your disk space by saving file data on your disk in the next available free areas. This means a file on your hard disk can occupy a number of different areas on the disk surface rather than one contiguous chunk. MS-DOS takes longer to read a fragmented file because it has to read different areas of your disk drive to find the entire file.

The Microsoft Defrag program arranges the files on your disk so they are all in one piece, making it faster to find and read a file.

Figure 28. Type "defrag" at the MS-DOS command line.

Figure 29. Select the drive you want to test for fragmentation.

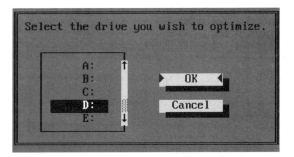

Figure 30. Defrag scans the directory of the current drive and reports the level of fragmentation of your data.

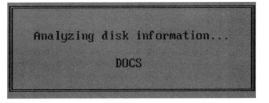

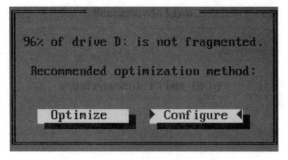

Figure 31. Defrag then recommends the method of optimization based on the level of fragmentation of the data on your disk. To begin optimizing with the recommended method, choose the *Optimize* button. If you want to configure the way you want your disk optimized, choose the *Configure* button.

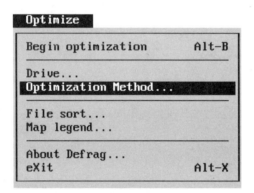

Figure 32. From the **Optimize** menu, choose the *Optimization Method* command.

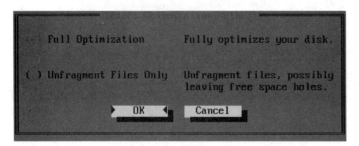

Figure 33. Defrag offers you two methods of optimization. *Full Optimization* defragments your entire disk, organizing files first and unused space last. *Unfragment Files Only* defragments all the files on your disk but at the expense of possibly leaving random clumps of free space on the disk.

Choose the optimization method that best suits you, keeping in mind that the *Full Optimization* takes longer.

Figure 34. As Defrag optimizes your data, it can also sort files into the order you select. Choose *File sort* from the **Optimize** menu to select the sort order for the files on your disk.

The *File Sort* dialog box offers you four methods of sorting your files with the option of ascending or descending order.

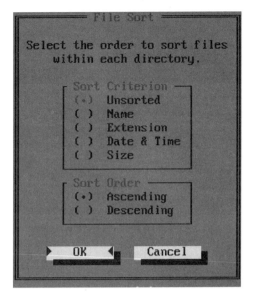

Figure 35. When you have finished configuring the way you want your data optimized, choose *Begin optimization* from the **Optimize** menu. Defrag displays, on the screen, a graphical simulation of the defragmentation procedure.

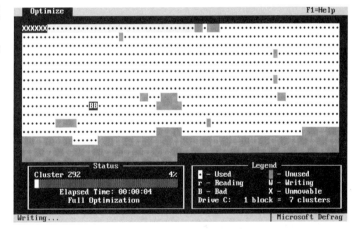

DoubleSpace Data Compression

MS-DOS 6 provides you with an excellent tool for making more disk space available. Microsoft DoubleSpace enables you to effectively double your disk space through the use of data compression.

DoubleSpace can also compress data on floppy disks to increase their capacity. Once created, a disk compressed using DoubleSpace performs like a normal disk drive.

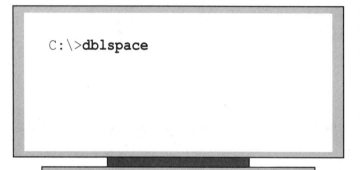

Figure 36. Type "dblspace" at the command prompt to start the Microsoft DoubleSpace program.

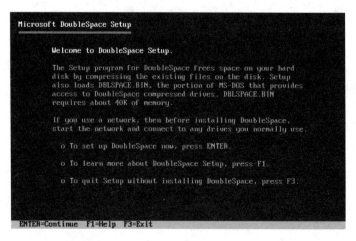

Figure 37. When you start DoubleSpace for the first time, it displays an information screen, telling you a little about the program and how it works. Press Enter to set up DoubleSpace.

Figure 38. There are two ways you can set up a compressed drive with DoubleSpace. Choose the *Express Setup* option and press Enter to let DoubleSpace compress your drive automatically with the default settings. See Figure 40 if you want to run the *Custom Setup*.

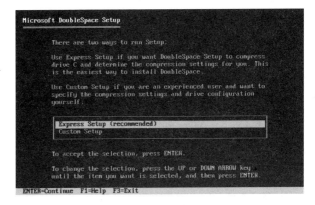

EXPRESS SETUP

Figure 39. DoubleSpace lets you know it is about to compress files and the amount of time the process will require. This may take a while and you cannot interrupt it. Press the Esc key to return to the previous screen or press C to create a compressed drive.

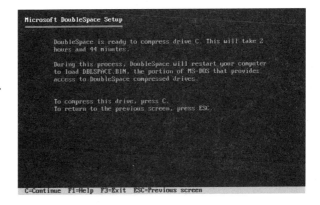

CUSTOM SETUP

The *Custom Setup* allows you a number of choices for setting up a compressed drive.

COMPRESS AN EXISTING DRIVE

Figure 40. Select *Compress an existing drive* to choose which disk drive you want to compress. This option is useful if the drive you select is quite full, because DoubleSpace increases the drive's capacity, leaving you more free space.

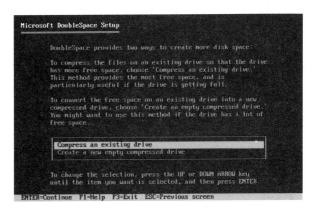

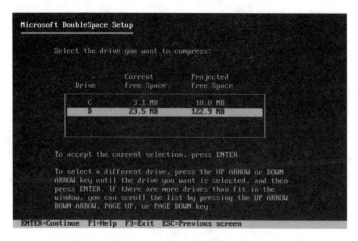

Figure 41. To compress the whole drive, choose a disk drive from the list.

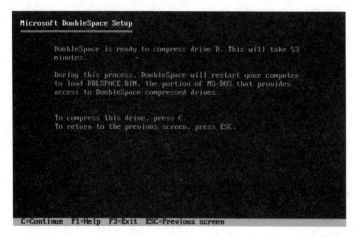

Figure 42. DoubleSpace gives you details of what it will do to your disk. Some files on your drive cannot be compressed—including your Windows swap file. Double-Space creates a drive with a new drive letter for these files. Change the *Free space on uncompressed drive:* figure to give yourself more free, uncompressed disk space. Select *Continue* and press Enter to accept the settings.

Figure 43. DoubleSpace lets you know it is about to compress files and how long it should take. Press Esc to cancel the process or C to continue.

CREATING A NEW DRIVE

Figure 44. Select *Create a new empty compressed drive* to create a compressed drive that appears as another drive letter.

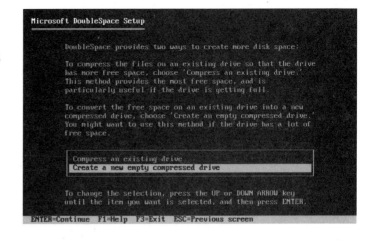

Figure 45. Select the drive on which you want to create the compressed disk. The drive you select will contain the compressed disk volume in a hidden file that you can delete only by using the DoubleSpace program.

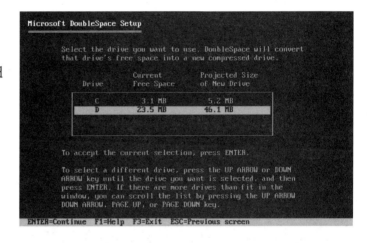

Figure 46. Before DoubleSpace creates the compressed drive, you can alter the default settings. If you want the compressed disk to use less space, then increase the amount of free space Double-Space leaves on the host disk. The compression ratio affects how accurately MS-DOS commands report the free space available on the compressed disk.

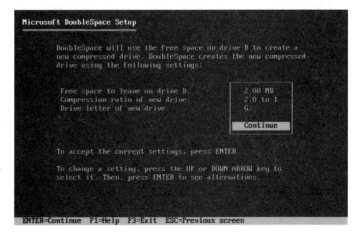

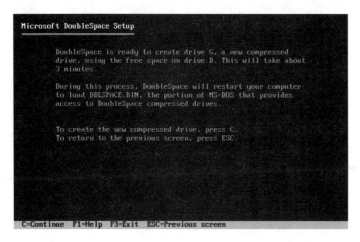

Figure 47. To create the compressed drive press C, or Esc if you want to exit. DoubleSpace first runs the *chkdsk* program on the host disk to ensure it is free of errors and then it creates the compressed disk.

CHANGING DRIVE SETTINGS

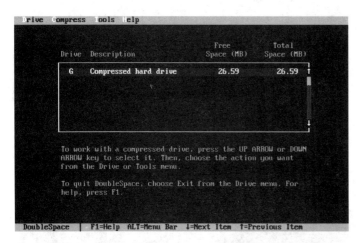

Figure 48. If you create any more compressed disks, DoubleSpace lists them as shown here each time you start the program.

Figure 49. Choose the *Info* command from the **Drive** menu, or use the arrow keys to select the compressed drive if there is more than one listed, then press Enter.

Figure 50. The *Info* dialog box shows you statistics for your compressed drive. The *Total space* figure shows the size of the compressed drive. *Total Space* is the sum of *Space used* and *Space free.*

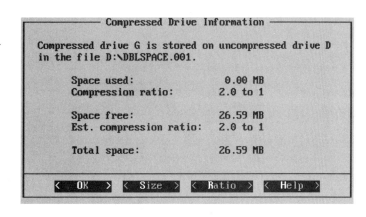

The *Compression ratio* is the average ratio of the data currently on the compressed disk. Double-Space uses the *Est. compression ratio* when it determines the amount of free space on the compressed disk.

Figure 51. To change the *Total space* for the compressed disk, choose the *Size* button. From the *Change Size* dialog box, you can adjust the free space on the host drive. You adjust the amount of free space available on the host drive to alter the size of the compressed drive.

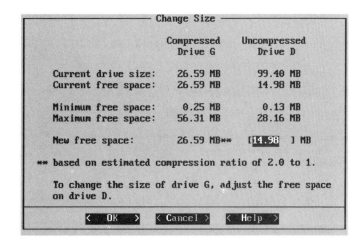

The more free space you allocate to the host drive, the less space is available for the compressed drive.

Figure 52. To change the *Est. compression ratio,* choose the *Ratio* button from Figure 50. Adjust the *New estimated compression ratio* to a figure that matches the type of data you will store on the compressed drive. Files such as text files and bitmaps (picture files) are more easily compressed than program files, so you can set the ratio higher.

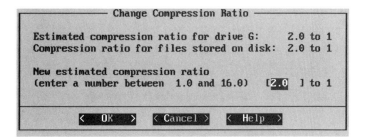

TOOLS

DoubleSpace has two tools for maintaining your compressed drives. *Defragment* produces similar results to the MS-DOS Defrag utility in the way that it organizes the data on your disk in a contiguous form. *Chkdsk* checks a compressed drive and can correct errors in the same way as the MS-DOS *chkdsk* command.

Figure 53. Choose *Defragment* from the **Tools** menu to open the *Defragment* dialog box.

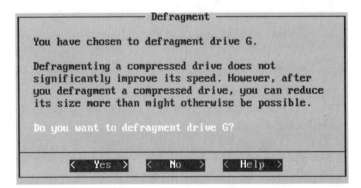

Figure 54. Although defragmenting the data on the compressed drive does not greatly improve its efficiency, sometimes Double-Space makes you run the defragment tool before you can reduce the size of a compressed drive.

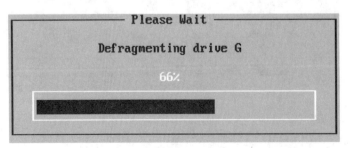

Figure 55. DoubleSpace shows you its progress as it defragments your compressed drive.

Figure 56. Choose *Chkdsk* from the **Tools** menu to open the *Chkdsk* dialog box. Choose the *Check* button if you want DoubleSpace to check the validity of your compressed drive. DoubleSpace asks you whether you want to fix any errors it comes across.

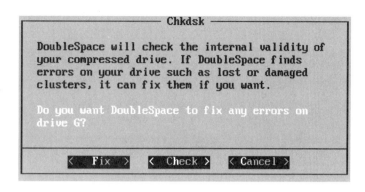

Choose the *Fix* button if you want the program to check and fix errors on the compressed drive.

FORMATTING A DRIVE

Figure 57. Choose *Format* from the **Drive** menu to display the *Format a Compressed Drive* dialog box. Only format a compressed drive if you want to clear its contents. Use this command with care as it erases all the data on the selected compressed drive.

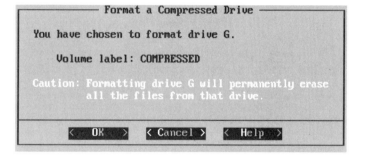

Figure 58. *Format* asks you again to confirm that you want to format the drive.

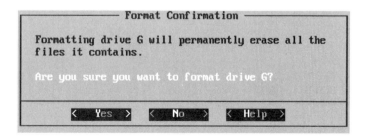

DELETING A DRIVE

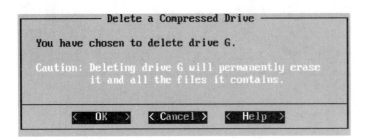

Figure 59. Choose *Delete* from the *Drive* menu to display the *Delete a Compressed Drive* dialog box. *Delete* erases all files on the compressed drive so make sure you have stored copies of any important files it contains.

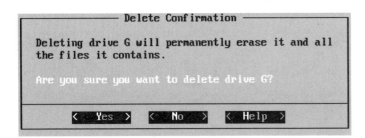

Figure 60. *Delete* prompts you again to confirm you want to delete the selected compressed drive and erase all the files it contains.

ADVANCED COMMAND TECHNIQUES

8

INTRODUCTION

This chapter is an extension of the basic MS-DOS commands covered in **Chapter 4, Command Line Survival.** It looks at various methods MS-DOS provides that allow you to use the command line more efficiently.

CONTROLLING OUTPUT

Most MS-DOS commands produce an output. For example, *dir* outputs a directory listing. *Format* outputs prompts and messages that you follow to format a disk.

This section covers two useful techniques you can adopt to control the output of data: redirecting and the *more* command.

REDIRECTING OUTPUT

You normally direct command output to your screen but you can redirect it to the printer or a file using a redirection character. The greater-than sign (>) is the most common. It redirects the output of a command to a file or device—usually a printer.

REDIRECTING TO A DEVICE

Figure 1. MS-DOS directs the command output to the port you specify after the redirection character. Adding ">LPTx" to the *dir* command prints a directory listing of C:\ exactly as it would appear on the screen. Using ">PRN" in the command sends the output to the printer on LPT1. "PRN" is used more widely.

```
C:\>dir>prn
```

```
c:\>type readme.txt>prn
```

Figure 2. This command prints the text file *readme.txt*; the >prn section of the command redirects the output to the printer.

REDIRECTING TO A FILE

You need to specify a filename when redirecting output to a file. MS-DOS creates the file if it does not already exist. If the file exists, MS-DOS replaces its contents with the current output.

```
c:\>chkdsk>b:\dskstats.txt
```

Figure 3. The command in this figure redirects the output of the *chkdsk* command to *b:\dskstats.txt.*

```
c:\>chkdsk>>b:\dskstats.txt
```

Figure 4. To append output to an existing file, use a much-greater-than sign (>>).

MORE COMMAND

Many MS-DOS commands produce an output that scrolls off the screen before you can read it. *Type, tree,* and *dir* are three examples. The *dir* command has switches (/p and /w) to control its output, but the other commands do not.

```
c:\>type readme.txt | more
```

Figure 5. You can control the output of these commands with the pipe (/) character and the *more* command. *More* displays the output of a command one screen at a time. You can generally type the pipe (/) character by pressing the Shift and Backslash keys.

Figure 6. *More* takes the output from the *type* command and displays it on screen. When *more* fills a screen, it interrupts *type* and shows the message "-- More --" at the bottom of the screen.

Press any key to see more of the output. To abort the command, you can type Ctrl+C.

COMMAND TEMPLATE

The command *template* enables you to edit and re-use the last command you entered. This can save you from re-entering the same command or one that is similar.

Figure 7. When you press Enter after typing in a command, MS-DOS copies the command to the template before executing it. If you press Esc, MS-DOS does not copy the command to the template and it does not execute the command. Pressing F5 copies the command to the template, but does not execute it.

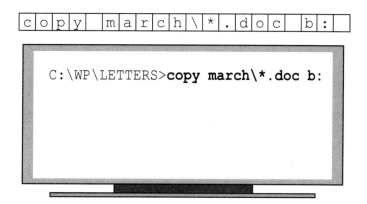

RE-USING THE LAST COMMAND

This procedure is useful when copying the same file onto several floppy disks. When you first key in the command and press Enter, MS-DOS copies the command to the template then executes the command.

Figure 8. Press F3 to repeat the command. MS-DOS copies the command stored in the template onto the command line. You then need only press Enter to execute the command.

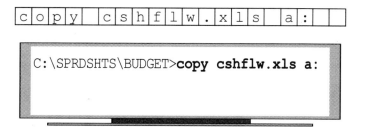

MODIFYING THE LAST COMMAND

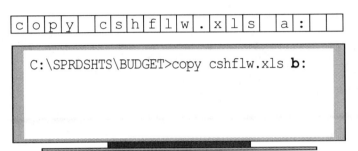

Figure 9. You can copy a command from the template and then modify it as required. This figure shows how to modify the *copy* command from the previous figure so you can copy the files to the B drive instead of the A drive.

First press F3 to display the last command on the command line. Press backspace twice to erase *a:* and type in *b:*. Pressing Enter executes the modified command and copies it to the template.

You can also use F3 to "graft" part of the last command onto a new command.

An example of grafting is to check files you want to delete with the *dir* command before deleting them. Enter the *dir* command to produce a list of the files to check that these are the ones you want to delete. When entered, MS-DOS stores the command in the template.

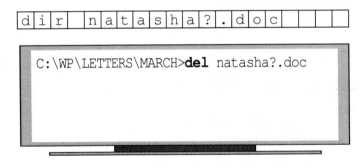

Figure 10. To graft the last command, type in *del* and press F3. MS-DOS inserts the command onto the command line. As you have typed three letters, the command from the template commences at the fourth letter, which is a space character.

Figure 11. The function key F1 copies single characters from the template. In this example, you need type *del* only, then F1 the required number of times, then 2, then F1, four more times.

Figure 12. F2 copies part of the command (see Figure 10) preceding a specific letter. The keystroke combination F2? inserts the command up to—but not including—the question mark. You can then insert 2 to replace the question mark. Pressing F3 completes the command.

Key in	F2?	2	F3
MS-DOS shows	dir natasha	2	.doc

Figure 13. F4 deletes part of a command that precedes a specific letter. You can then use the Insert key to insert text into the template and the command line simultaneously.

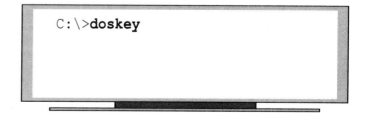

This example changes the *dir* command shown in the template to a *copy* command using the same file reference. To do this, press F4 four times to delete the first four characters in the command. Turn on Insert mode by pressing the Insert key. Type *copy* and a space directly onto the command line. Use F3 to copy the rest of the command from the template.

Using Doskey

You can use the Doskey program to keep a record of about 35 commands; the exact figure depends on the average size of the commands. Once you reach the limit, Doskey discards the oldest command so that it can record the newest.

You can view or use any of these commands at any time when you activate Doskey. In addition, Doskey provides command editing facilities.

Figure 14. Doskey occupies about 4 kb of memory. To install the program, type *doskey* at the command prompt as shown.

```
C:\>doskey
cd \dos
dir *.txt
copy readme.txt notes.doc
ren notes.doc amazing.txt
del amazing.txt
```

Figure 15. To illustrate Doskey, type in the commands shown. Note that the first command installs Doskey itself.

```
1:  cd \dos
2:  dir *.txt
3:  copy readme.txt notes.doc
4:  ren notes.doc amazing.txt
5:  del amazing.txt
```

Figure 16. Pressing the function key F7 displays a full list of the commands entered since you installed Doskey.

```
C:\>del amazing.txt
```

Figure 17. Press the Up Arrow key to see the last command entered. Pressing Enter executes it.

```
C:\>copy readme.txt notes.doc
```

Figure 18. Pressing the Up Arrow key twice more displays the third command you entered.

```
C:\>ren notes.doc amazing.txt
```

Figure 19. Press the Down Arrow key and Doskey displays the fourth command in the list.

```
C:\>cd \dos
```

Figure 20. The Page Up key shows the first command in the list.

Figure 21. The Page Down key displays the last command in the list.

```
C:\>del amazing.txt
```

Figure 22. Use F8 to search for commands. For example, type *co* then press F8 to display a command starting with "co." Pressing F8 repeatedly displays, in order, any other commands starting with "co."

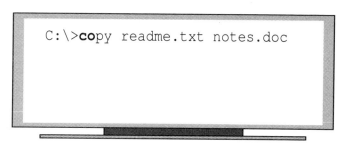

```
C:\>copy readme.txt notes.doc
```

Figure 23. You can use F9 to display a command from the command list. Press F7 to view the command list and then F9. MS-DOS displays *Line number* to which you key in the number of the command you want. For example, *4* displays the fourth command in the list.

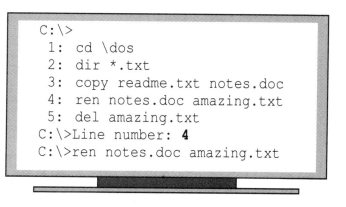

```
C:\>
 1: cd \dos
 2: dir *.txt
 3: copy readme.txt notes.doc
 4: ren notes.doc amazing.txt
 5: del amazing.txt
C:\>Line number: 4
C:\>ren notes.doc amazing.txt
```

With Doskey you can place several commands at the command line and enter them as one command. Pressing Ctrl+T inserts a paragraph mark (¶) that separates commands. Doskey accepts as many commands as you require, providing you type fewer than 128 characters.

Figure 24. The commands shown here copy *letter2.doc* to the *april* directory then delete it from the original directory.

```
C:\WP\LETTERS>copy letter2.doc
april¶del letter2.doc
```

EDITING COMMANDS WITH DOSKEY

Doskey gives you editing facilities that are similar to the MS-DOS Editor.

Key	Moves the cursor
Left Arrow	one character to the left
Right Arrow	one character to the right
Ctrl+Left Arrow	one word left
Ctrl+Right Arrow	one word right
Home	to the beginning of the command
End	to the end of the command

Figure 25. When you install Doskey, you can move the cursor over the command to where you want to make the alteration. The table outlines the effect of cursor movement keys.

Key	Moves the cursor
Backspace	deletes the character to the left of the cursor
Del	deletes the character at the cursor
Ins	turns Insert mode off or on
Esc	clears the command from the command line

Figure 26. This table shows the functions of some of the other keys when used with Doskey.

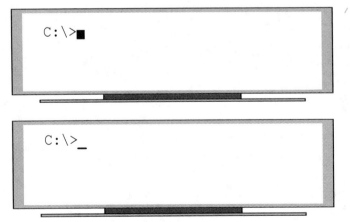

```
C:\>■
```

Figure 27. When you have activated it, Insert mode lets you type text between existing text. MS-DOS displays the cursor as a small block.

```
C:\>_
```

Figure 28. Overtype mode shows the cursor as an underscore and replaces text in the command line. Press the Ins key to toggle between the two modes.

MACROS

You often use certain commands or command sequences repeatedly. These commands can involve quite complex path names and switches. Because entering these is time-consuming and error-prone, it is more efficient to define a macro.

A macro is a command or a set of commands that you name. With Doskey, you can define DOS command line macros. Once you have defined a macro, all you need to do is key in its name and MS-DOS executes the commands.

DEFINING MACROS

Figure 29. In this example, we are using Doskey to define the macro named "dirlet," which we have defined as listing the contents of the *wp\letters* directory.

```
C:\>doskey dirlet=dir c:\wp\letters
```

As an example, let us presume that at regular intervals you run a listing of the *letters* directory to view its contents. Rather than enter the *dir* command and path each time, you can save the entire command as a one-word, easy-to-remember macro.

Figure 30. To run the dirlet macro, you simply enter its name at the DOS prompt and press Enter, as you would with any other command. MS-DOS then executes, in turn, each command specified in the macro.

```
C:\>dirlet
Volume in drive C is MS-DOS
Volume Serial Number is 1728-71FC
Directory of C:\WP\LETTERS

.            <DIR>          04-01-93   2:15p
..           <DIR>          05-01-93   2:15p
MAY      DOC      5438 06-05-93   3.52p
MILKMAN  DOC       398 07-05-93   2.56p
CMPLAINT DOC      2244 08-05-93   4.26p
JUNE     DOC      3386 09-06-93   8.02a
AUGUST   DOC      8834 10-08-93   9:16a
```

```
C:\>dirlet
Volume in drive C is MS-DOS
Volume Serial Number is 1728-71FC
Directory of C:\WP\LETTERS

.           <DIR>         04-01-93    2:15p
..          <DIR>         05-01-93    2:15p
MAY         <DIR>         06-11-93   10:32a
JUNE        <DIR>         06-11-93   11:02a
JULY        <DIR>         06-11-93   11:26a
AUG         <DIR>         06-11-93   12:45p
```

Figure 31. The dirlet macro we have defined is appropriate if you need to list the *letters* directory only. The dirlet macro in this example no longer provides the information you need because we have moved all the files in the *letters* directory to subdirectories.

```
C:\>doskey dirlet=dir c:\wp\letters\$1
```

Figure 32. Rather than create a macro to list the contents for every subdirectory, you can redefine the dirlet macro so that you can type in the one you want. The **$1** is a place holder for any parameter (in this case a subdirectory name) that you specify after the dirlet macro command. Up to nine parameters ($1–$9) can be used in a macro.

```
C:\>dirlet may
Volume in drive C is MS-DOS
Volume Serial Number is 1728-71FC
Directory of C:\WP\LETTERS\MAY

.           <DIR>               04-01-93    2:15p
..          <DIR>               05-01-93    2:15p
MAY       DOC      5438         06-05-93    3.52p
MILKMAN   DOC       398         07-05-93    2.56p
CMPLAINT  DOC      2244         08-05-93    4.26p
```

Figure 33. This figure shows the output from the dirlet macro when we have used the directory name *may* as a parameter.

Figure 34. If you omit the parameter when running the dirlet macro, you will be given a listing of the *wp\letters* directory. MS-DOS substitutes the $1 command in the macro with a blank.

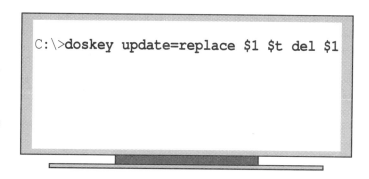

```
C:\>dirlet
```

Figure 35. You can write a macro only one line long so in order to include additional commands on the one line, you must use a separator. The **$t** character (short for Ctrl+T) separates commands in the macro. In this case, the macro contains two commands: the *replace* command and the *del* command.

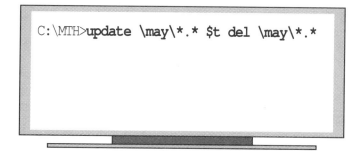

```
C:\>doskey update=replace $1 $t del $1
```

Figure 36. The *update* macro from the previous figure replaces files with the same name in the current directory, called *mth*, with files from the *may* directory, which it then deletes.

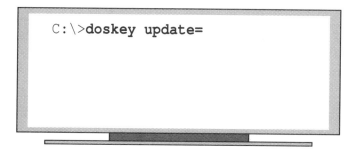

```
C:\MTH>update \may\*.* $t del \may\*.*
```

DELETING MACROS

Figure 37. If you want to delete a macro, enter its name with an equals sign after the *Doskey* command and press the Enter key. In this example, MS-DOS will remove the *update* macro from memory, allowing more space for new macros.

```
C:\>doskey update=
```

SAVING MACROS

Since macros are stored in your computer's RAM, switching off the computer destroys all macros. One method of saving macros is to store them in a file for reloading when you next start your computer.

```
C:\>doskey /macros
dirlet=dir c:\wp\letters\$1
update=replace $1 $t del $1
```

Figure 38. Use the */macros* switch with the *Doskey* command if you want to list macros.

```
C:\>doskey /macros > macros.bat
```

Figure 39. In this example, we are redirecting the output of the *Doskey* */macros* command to a file. To do this, you use the */macros* switch with the greater-than (>) sign and a filename. Here, all macro definitions are written to the file *macros.bat*.

```
doskey dirlet=dir c:\wp\letters\$1
doskey update=replace $1 $t del $1
```

Figure 40. The */macros* switch outputs only the definition of the macros. To enable the macros to be re-loaded, you must insert the *Doskey* command before each macro shown in the file *macros.bat*. Refer to the following section on batch files for details of running a batch file such as *macros.bat*.

BATCH FILES

The main difference between batch files and macros is that batch files are stored on disk whereas macros reside in RAM. Macros run much faster but may be lost when you turn power off. Also, you can include any number of commands in a batch program, whereas you are limited to 127 characters in defining a macro.

Figure 41. You typically use batch files to perform a sequence of repetitive tasks, such as loading macros, running simple demonstrations, installing applications, and backing up and restoring documents. MS-DOS identifies batch files by their extension "*bat*."

```
C:\>dir bin\*.bat

DIRLET    BAT     349  01-04-93   3:50p
ADDPATH   BAT     223  02-06-93   1:31p
UPDATE    BAT     551  04-07-93   1:47a
MACROS    BAT     226  06-08-93  12:00p
```

Figure 42. To run a batch file, simply enter its name at the DOS prompt and press Enter. You do not need to enter the *bat* extension.

```
C:\>macros.bat
doskey dirlet=dir c:\wp\letters\$1
doskey update=replace $1 $t del $1
```

PARAMETERS

You can use parameters in batch files the same way you use them in macros. The only difference is that batch files use the percent (%) symbol to identify a parameter, whereas macros use the dollar ($) symbol.

Figure 43. In this batch program, *update.bat*, we have used the parameters %1 and %2 to allow the entry of the source filename(s) and destination path.

```
C:\>type update.bat
replace %1 %2
del %1
```

BATCH FILE COMMANDS

In addition to the commands you have already encountered, MS-DOS includes a number of commands specifically designed for batch programs.

```
echo a Apples
echo b Oranges
choice /c:ab Make a choice
```

Figure 44. This figure shows the batch file, *fruit.bat*, with two options, *Apples* and *Oranges*, and the *choice* command as the last line.

```
C:\>fruit

a Apples
b Oranges
Make a choice[A,B]?
```

Figure 45. When you run the batch file, *Choice* shows the specified prompt to enable a user to choose from the list of items, in this case *Apples* and *Oranges*.

```
echo Please insert a disk in drive A
```

Figure 46. The *echo* command allows you to display messages on the screen.

```
@dir
```

Figure 47. You can prevent a command from being echoed to the screen by placing the "@" symbol in front of it.

Figure 48. To display each command before execution, turn echo on as shown here. Alternatively, if you do not want to display each command, use *echo off.*

```
echo on
```

Figure 49. The *for* command enables you to execute commands on a set of files or text strings. The command in this figure uses *find* to search for the text string "MS-DOS" in all files with the DOC and TXT extension. *Find* lists each occurrence of the string.

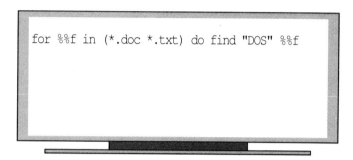

```
for %%f in (*.doc *.txt) do find "DOS" %%f
```

Figure 50. Use the *if* command with the *goto* command to test for a condition and jump to another part of a batch file.

```
if %1==readme.txt goto option1
```

Figure 51. The *pause* command shows the message "Press any key to continue . . ." on the screen and waits for a keypress. This command is useful when waiting for the user, for example, to insert a disk into a drive.

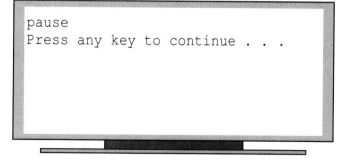

```
pause
Press any key to continue . . .
```

SAMPLE BATCH FILE

```
C:\>type mailbak.bat
@echo off
rem This batch file backs up DOC files
cls
cd \wp\letters
echo Insert the MAIL back up disk in A
pause
xcopy *.doc a: /s /m
```

Figure 52. Use the *type* command if you want to see the contents of a batch file, such as *mailbak.bat* shown here.

See Figure 53 for a description of this batch file.

Figure 53. This table explains the purpose of each of the commands in the batch file *mailbak.bat*.

Batch Command	Purpose/Explanation
@echo off	Precludes the display of a command on the screen as it is executed.
rem This batch file backs up DOC files	Use the rem (remark) statement to describe the use of the batch file or comment on commands it contains.
cls	Clears the screen.
cd \wp\letters	Change to the wp\letters directory.
echo Insert the MAIL backup disk in A	Prompts the operator to insert a disk in the A drive.
pause	Displays the message "Press any key to continue ..." and waits for a keypress.
xcopy *.doc a: /s /m	Copy files that have not been modified since the last backup from the current directory, including subdirectories, to the A drive.

CUSTOMIZING YOUR PC 9

STARTUP

Switching on a personal computer starts a series of internal checks before MS-DOS loads. If you have a system disk in floppy drive A or B, the computer loads MS-DOS from that disk. Otherwise it loads MS-DOS from drive C. DOS refers to the drive from which you load MS-DOS as the "boot disk."

Once loaded, MS-DOS looks for two important files in the root directory of the boot disk—*config.sys* and *autoexec.bat*. Both files contain commands which MS-DOS executes before displaying the command prompt, DOS Shell, or a menu.

Config.sys contains a list of configuration commands. It performs a variety of tasks including controlling the input and output devices that you connect to the computer.

Autoexec.bat is a batch file containing various startup commands. It determines the procedure MS-DOS follows when you start your computer.

You can alter these two files to configure and customize your computer to suit your requirements.

CONFIG.SYS FILE

Figure 1. The commands in *config.sys* load devices that you can install and reserves memory space to process data.

MS-DOS reads *config.sys* during the startup process. It stores the commands in memory so it can access them when it needs to.

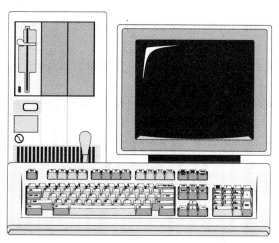

A basic config.sys for an XT computer

```
buffers=10
files=8
break=on
device=c:\mouse\mouse.sys
country=061,437,c:\dos\country.sys
```

A basic config.sys for a 286 computer

```
buffers=10
files=20
device=c:\dos\himem.sys
dos=high
break=on
device=c:\mouse\mouse.sys
device=c:\dos\ramdrive.sys   1024
country=061,437,c:\dos\country.sys
```

A basic config.sys for a 386 (or higher) computer

```
buffers=10
files=20
device=c:\dos\himem.sys
device=c:\dos\emm386.exe   noems
dos=high,UMB
break=on
devicehigh=c:\mouse\mouse.sys
devicehigh=c:\dos\ramdrive.sys   1024
country=061,437,c:\dos\country.sys
```

Figure 2. This figure shows three examples of basic *config.sys* files: one each for an XT, a 286, and a 386 (or higher) machine. You should base your *config.sys* file on the type of machine you have.

The following list outlines who and what usually customizes a *config.sys* file:

• the dealer from whom you bought the equipment;

• you, when recommended in the installation manual of a particular product;

• the setup program you purchased with a new product, such as a mouse; and

• the MS-DOS Setup program that installed MS-DOS 6.

The following sections explain the different commands listed in these three *config.sys* files.

BUFFERS

Buffers are temporary storage areas in memory. MS-DOS uses buffers to store data when it needs to read and write to a disk.

Figure 3. Which *buffers* command you insert into the *config.sys* file depends on how much RAM you have in your computer.

The *buffers* command in this figure sets aside 10 buffers, each with 512 bytes of RAM.

```
buffers=10
```

FILES

Figure 4. The *files* command in *config.sys* controls how many files you can simultaneously open. You can set this to between 8 and 255 files.

If you do not have a *files* command in your *config.sys* file, MS-DOS defaults to 8 files.

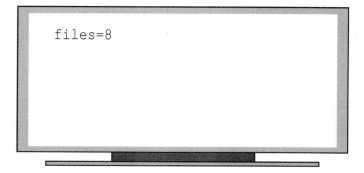

```
files=8
```

MEMORY MANAGERS

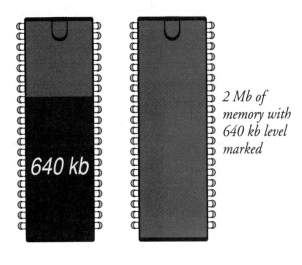

2 Mb of memory with 640 kb level marked

Figure 5. MS-DOS, by itself, cannot access more than the first 640 kb of RAM. To use memory above the 640 kb barrier, MS-DOS needs the help of a program called a "memory manager." MS-DOS supplies *himem.sys* as a memory manager and you can load it using the *config.sys* file during startup.

To fully understand this section, you should make sure you have read the **Types of Memory** section in Chapter 2.

```
device=c:\dos\himem.sys
```

Figure 6. The *device* command shown here loads *himem.sys* as the memory manager.

When MS-DOS needs to use extended memory, either to store or retrieve data, it calls on the Himem program to do this.

```
device=c:\dos\emm386.exe   noems
```

Figure 7. Use this command only on 386 (or higher) PCs. It tells MS-DOS to store device drivers and TSR (*terminate and stay resident*) programs in the upper memory area.

Using this command frees conventional memory that your programs can use.

The command consists of two parts as follows:

- *c:\dos\emm386.exe* is the path statement MS-DOS uses to find the file *emm386.exe*.

- *noems* disables expanded memory (ems) so that MS-DOS can access the upper memory area. Alternatively, you can set a limit stating the number of kilobytes that MS-DOS can use to store such things as drivers.

LOADING DOS HIGH

Figure 8. The MS-DOS operating system normally takes up about 60 kb of conventional memory.

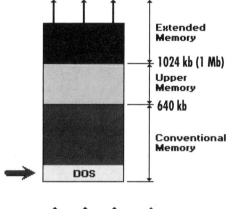

Figure 9. You can load some of MS-DOS into a part of extended memory called the *high memory area* (HMA) to free more conventional memory for applications. The HMA comprises the first 64 kb of extended memory.

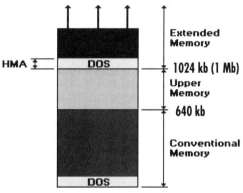

Figure 10. Specify the command *dos=high* in your *config.sys* file to make sure DOS runs in the high memory area.

```
dos=high
```

Use this command on a 286 (or higher) PC that has more than 640 kb of conventional memory. You must insert *himem.sys* in the *config.sys* file in a line before this command.

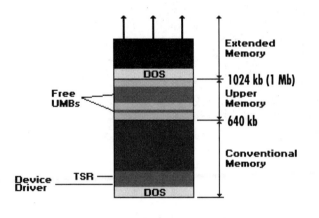

Figure 11. The *upper memory blocks* (UMBs) are part of the 384 kb of upper memory area above the standard 640 kb of memory.

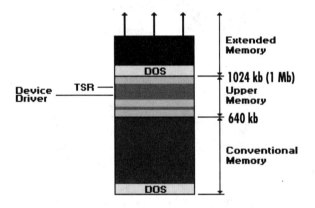

Figure 12. You can use the free UMBs for running device drivers and TSR programs.

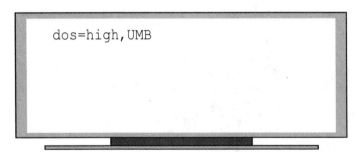

```
dos=high,UMB
```

Figure 13. The *UMB* parameter in the *dos=high* command lets you load device drivers and TSR programs into UMBs. You can load device drivers into this area using *devicehigh=* commands. See the following **Device Drivers** section for more details.

You must put the *himem.sys* and *emm386.exe* commands in the *config.sys* file before *dos=high, UMB* to use this option.

BREAK

Figure 14. Pressing Ctrl+C or Ctrl+Break stops a program. The *break* command in *config.sys* controls how often MS-DOS checks to see if you have pressed these keys.

```
break=on
```

Break=on prompts MS-DOS to check more often, but slows the system down. The default command is *break=off,* which applies if you leave the command out of *config.sys.*

DEVICE DRIVERS

For MS-DOS to recognize a device, it must have a program called a device driver. MS-DOS contains built-in device drivers for the keyboard, video monitor, and disk drives.

Figure 15. You must install software device drivers to use other devices, such as a mouse. When you buy the device, it comes with a setup disk containing the device driver, which you need to install onto your hard disk.

Figure 16. This figure shows a directory listing of the three mouse standard files on a setup disk. *Mouse.sys* contains the device driver. *Readme.doc* contains updates to the manual. The setup program in this case is in *setup.exe.* Some devices name the setup program *install.exe.*

```
A:\>dir
Volume in drive A is MOUSE-SETUP
Directory of A:\
MOUSE     SYS    14518  12-05-93   4:00a
README    DOC     8224  12-05-93   4:00a
SETUP     EXE    23418  12-05-93   4:00p
            3 file(s)
```

```
A:\>setup

Create directory C:\MOUSE? [y/n] y
SETUP is creating directory C:\MOUSE
SETUP is copying MOUSE.SYS to directory
C:\MOUSE
Update CONFIG.SYS? [y/n] y
SETUP has updated your CONFIG.SYS file.
Installation is complete. You should reboot
your computer so that MS-DOS can recognize
your mouse.
Reboot now? [y/n] y
```

Figure 17. A typical setup program creates a directory for the device driver and copies the driver into that directory. Setup then adds a *device* command to *config.sys*.

```
DEVICE=C:\MOUSE\MOUSE.SYS
```

Figure 18. You need to reboot your system so that MS-DOS can execute the *device* command. If your system uses *dos=high, UMB*, insert *devicehigh* instead of *device* in the command.

When MS-DOS reads a *device* command, it can find the specified driver and load it into memory. MS-DOS does not actually recognize that this driver is for a mouse. Programs know that it is a mouse driver and relay messages from the mouse to MS-DOS.

Most setup programs install drivers into directories with the same name as the device. For example, this figure shows *mouse.sys* in *c:\mouse*. The directory you use is of no significance to MS-DOS whatsoever. It simply ensures that a setup program can replace an older version of the driver with a newer version.

If you copy the device driver to another directory, be sure to change the *device* command in *config.sys* to reflect the new location.

RAM DRIVE

A RAM drive sets part of extended RAM aside for MS-DOS to use as a simulated disk drive. MS-DOS provides *ramdrive.sys* to control the RAM drive. Using a RAM drive can reduce processing time—especially with applications that create a number of temporary files.

Data in a RAM drive is stored only temporarily. You can copy it for permanent storage on disk.

Figure 19. The device command in this figure sets the path to *ramdrive.sys* and the size of the RAM drive at one megabyte (1024 kb).

```
device=c:\dos\ramdrive.sys  1024
```

NATIONAL LANGUAGE FORMAT

Different countries write dates, times, currency values, and decimals in different forms. If your computer is not using a format suitable for your country, you can select the correct format with *country.sys*.

Figure 20. The *country* command tells MS-DOS which conventions to use. MS-DOS uses U.S. conventions by default. The *country* command has three parameters that you separate with commas:

```
country=061,437,c:\dos\country.sys
```

- The *country* code is the number of the country. 061 refers to International English. Your MS-DOS manual has a complete list of country codes.
- The *default page code* sets the number of characters that you can print or display on the screen. Use 437 for the United States, the United Kingdom, and Australia.
- The *path statement* lets DOS find the *country.sys* file.

MODIFYING CONFIG.SYS

You can modify *config.sys* with the MS-DOS text editor. However, *config.sys* is a critical system file so, before altering it, you should take some precautions. An error in this file could make your system unusable.

If you follow the strategy described below, you can always put the system back the way it was before you made the changes.

- Make a system disk. You can use this disk to reboot the system if anything goes wrong.
- Make a backup copy of *config.sys* on your hard disk. Call it *config.bak*. You can rename *config.bak* to *config.sys* if you make changes to the original *config.sys* file that it turns out you don't want.

With these precautions, you have two ways of restoring your system to its original state if anything goes wrong.

The MS-DOS Editor enables you to edit your *config.sys* file. You can insert, modify, or delete the commands outlined in this chapter. The MS-DOS manual contains other commands that you can insert into *config.sys*.

AUTOEXEC.BAT FILE

MS-DOS executes *autoexec.bat* in the last stage of the boot process. It contains one or more commands that tell MS-DOS how to start up your computer each time you turn it on.

You can modify *autoexec.bat* to suit your needs. As *autoexec.bat* is a batch file, you make changes to it in the same way as you change any batch file (see **Chapter 8, Advanced Command Techniques**).

Figure 21. This figure shows a typical *autoexec.bat* file. These are just a few examples of the commands you can include.

The following figures explain the contents of this file.

```
@echo off
prompt $p$g
path  c:\;c:\dos;c:\windows;c:\word
smartdrv.exe
rem doskey
call macros
set temp=c:\temp
mouse
dosshell
```

Figure 22. *@echo off* stops MS-DOS from displaying the DOS prompt and commands before MS-DOS executes them.

The @ character in front of the command prevents MS-DOS from displaying the *echo off* command itself.

```
@echo off
```

Figure 23. *Prompt pg* configures the command line prompt to show the current directory (*$p*) followed by the " > " sign (*$g*). The result is that MS-DOS displays the prompt as "C:\DOS>", for example.

```
prompt $p$g
```

Figure 24. The path statement in *autoexec.bat* sets the MS-DOS search path. Insert a search path so that MS-DOS can find frequently used files from the directories you specify.

```
path  c:\;c:\dos;c:\windows;c:\word
```

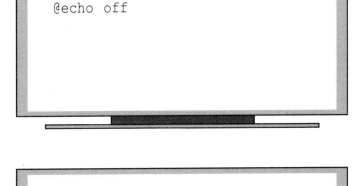

A path statement can contain one or more directories. Separate each directory in the path with a semicolon.

MS-DOS searches the directories in the order in which they appear in the path statement. Speed up your system by placing the most commonly used directories at the beginning.

DISK CACHE CONTROLLERS

A disk cache is a part of RAM which stores data that MS-DOS has recently accessed from disk. It can improve the performance of a computer by reducing the number of disk operations MS-DOS has to perform.

If you use a disk cache, MS-DOS searches it for data before searching a disk. If it finds the information required, it does not need to search the disk. Therefore a cache can reduce processing time.

MS-DOS supplies *smartdrv.exe* as a disk cache controller. The cache controller tells MS-DOS that it is holding data in RAM. MS-DOS reads as much data from, and writes as much data to, the disk cache as it can. During idle stages, MS-DOS writes the data stored in the cache to appropriate parts of the disk.

Figure 25. Specify *smartdrv.exe* as a line in your ***autoexec.bat*** file to load the disk cache program.

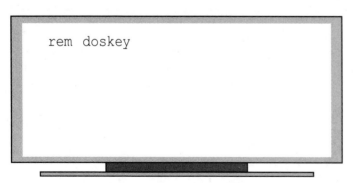

Figure 26. The *rem* (remark) command de-activates a command, in this case the *doskey* command. Most people de-activate rather than delete commands when they no longer need them.

You can re-activate the command by deleting *rem*.

Figure 27. A *call* command in a batch file executes another batch file and returns to the first one.

The *call macros* command in this figure runs the macro batch file then returns and continues processing the commands in *autoexec.bat*.

```
call macros
```

Figure 28. With the *set temp* command, you determine where you want MS-DOS to save temporary files.

This example sets the temp directory as *c:\temp*. Setting the RAM drive as the temp directory speeds up processing.

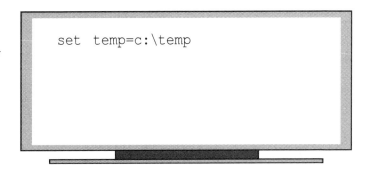

```
set temp=c:\temp
```

Figure 29. This command loads the *mouse.com* device driver into memory. This is a similar process to loading *mouse.sys* device drivers with *config.sys*.

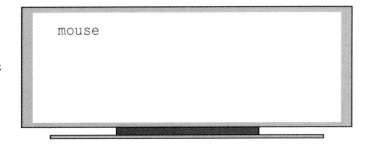

```
mouse
```

Figure 30. The *dosshell* command activates the DOS Shell program. When MS-DOS has finished processing *autoexec.bat*, the DOS Shell appears on the screen.

```
dosshell
```

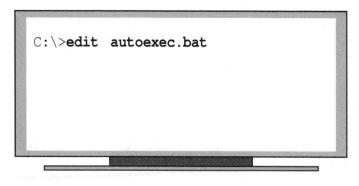

```
C:\>edit autoexec.bat
```

Figure 31. At the DOS prompt type "edit autoexec.bat" to modify an *autoexec.bat* file. This starts the MS-DOS Editor and loads *autoexec.bat*. You can then make the necessary changes and save the file.

For MS-DOS to recognize the modified version of *autoexec.bat*, you must reboot your computer.

OPTIMIZING MEMORY

MemMaker reorganizes memory-resident programs (TSRs) and device drivers to make the most of your system's memory.

You can use MemMaker if your system contains an 80386 or 80486 processor.

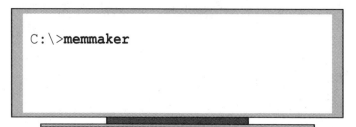

```
C:\>memmaker
```

Figure 32. To start MemMaker, type "memmaker" at the MS-DOS prompt.

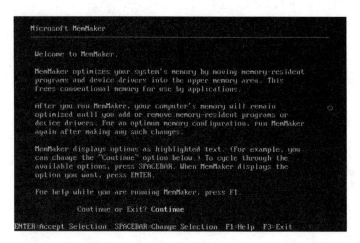

Figure 33. MemMaker begins with an introduction screen. Press the F3 key to exit, or Enter if you want to run MemMaker.

Figure 34. Choose the *Express* setup if you want MemMaker to alter your system configuration. If you want to customize the settings, choose the *Custom* setup. Use the Spacebar to change between *Express* and *Custom* setups and press Enter to accept the selection.

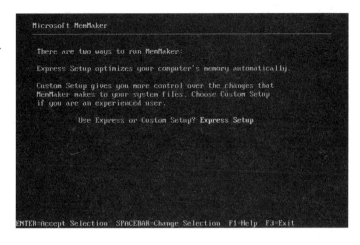

Figure 35. Some programs you use may require expanded mem-ory (EMS). Look at the documentation for your programs if you are not sure which type of memory they need.

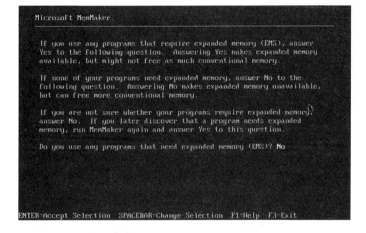

Figure 36. The *Custom* setup lets you select which programs and device drivers you want Mem-Maker to reorganize and the additional regions of memory it can use.

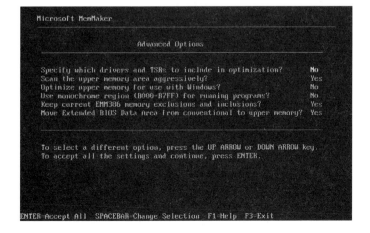

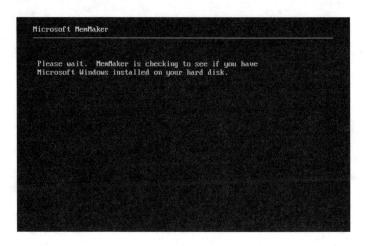

Figure 37. MemMaker searches the directories on your system for Microsoft Windows.

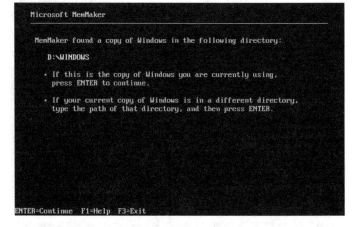

Figure 38. If you have Microsoft Windows on your system, the *Custom* setup allows you to enter an alternative directory path if you are running multiple versions of Windows.

Figure 39. MemMaker prompts you to press Enter so it can restart your computer to determine which device drivers and memory-resident programs (TSRs) you currently have installed.

Figure 40. After your system re-starts, there is a slight pause as MemMaker calculates the best way it can use your computer's memory to run the device drivers and memory-resident programs.

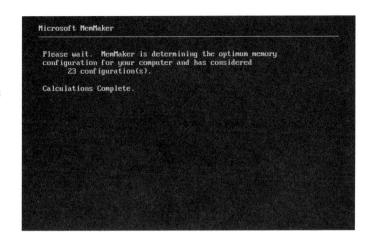

Figure 41. MemMaker edits your system files, *autoexec.bat*, and *config.sys* with the new settings for the device drivers and memory-resident programs.

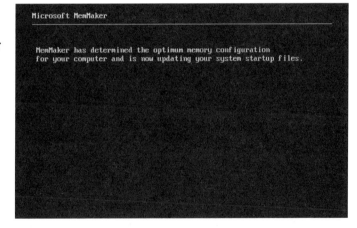

Figure 42. Press Enter to make MemMaker restart your computer, this time with the new configurations it applied to your system files. Look carefully for any unusual messages on the screen as your system restarts.

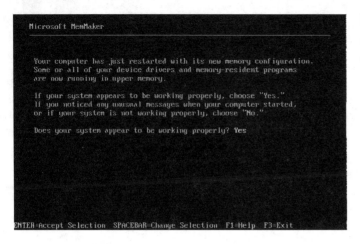

```
Microsoft MemMaker

Your computer has just restarted with its new memory configuration.
Some or all of your device drivers and memory-resident programs
are now running in upper memory.

If your system appears to be working properly, choose "Yes."
If you noticed any unusual messages when your computer started,
or if your system is not working properly, choose "No."

Does your system appear to be working properly? Yes

ENTER=Accept Selection  SPACEBAR=Change Selection  F1=Help  F3=Exit
```

Figure 43. After your system restarts, MemMaker asks if your system is working correctly. Select *Yes* if you did not see any unusual messages when your system restarted.

```
Microsoft MemMaker

MemMaker has finished optimizing your system's memory. The following
table summarizes the memory use (in bytes) on your system:

                              Before       After
Memory Type                   MemMaker     MemMaker     Change

Free conventional memory:     545,984      628,160      82,176

Upper memory:
    Used by programs          82,736       118,992      36,256
    Reserved for Windows      0            0            0
    Reserved for EMS          0            0            0
    Free                      55,536       19,280

Expanded memory:              Disabled     Disabled

Your original CONFIG.SYS and AUTOEXEC.BAT files have been saved
as CONFIG.UMB and AUTOEXEC.UMB.  If MemMaker changed your Windows
SYSTEM.INI file, the original file was saved as SYSTEM.UMB.

ENTER=Exit  ESC=Undo changes
```

Figure 44. MemMaker shows you statistics on the conventional memory you have gained compared with the conventional memory your system used before you ran MemMaker. Press Enter to return to the MS-DOS prompt.

WINDOWS PROGRAMS 10

WINDOWS PROGRAMS

MS-DOS 6 has, for the first time, provided several programs specifically designed for use with Microsoft Windows. There are three Windows programs: *Anti-Virus, Backup,* and *Undelete.*

These programs are Windows versions of MS-DOS-specific programs. In other words, you can run the MS-DOS version or the Windows version of *Backup*—whichever is more convenient for you.

Figure 1. When you install MS-DOS on your system, you are asked whether you would like to install Windows versions of *Anti-Virus, Backup,* and *Undelete.* If you install the Windows versions, MS-DOS creates a new program group, *Microsoft Tools,* in your Program Manager.

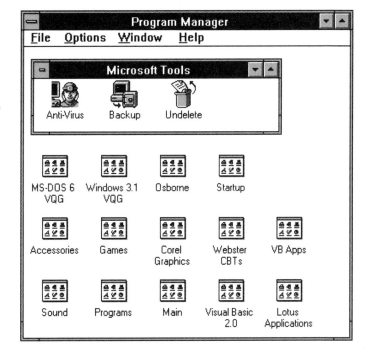

ANTI-VIRUS

Anti-Virus is a program designed to protect your system from viruses, or to detect and remove a virus that may have already infected your system. For more details about viruses, see **Chapter 7, In Charge of Your System.**

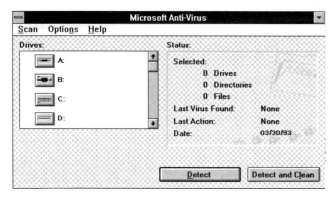

Figure 2. This figure illustrates the Anti-Virus startup screen. This screen allows you to set options and to select a disk drive to scan for viruses.

SELECTING A DRIVE

In Figure 2, the disk drives available on your computer are listed on the left-hand side of the dialog box. To select a drive (you may have to scroll through a list), you click on the drive icon.

You can select multiple drives by clicking on as many drives as you want.

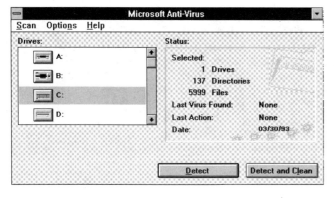

Figure 3. After you select a drive to scan, Anti-Virus tells you on the right-hand side of the dialog box how many directories and files are on the drive.

STARTING THE SCAN

Anti-Virus provides two options for detecting and removing viruses—*Detect* or *Detect and Clean*. These options are the same except that *Detect and Clean* is simply more automatic. Selecting *Detect and Clean* means that your system removes detected viruses automatically, whereas Anti-Virus prompts you if you select *Detect*.

Figure 4. The first step Anti-Virus takes to detect viruses is to check memory, an area where viruses often lurk.

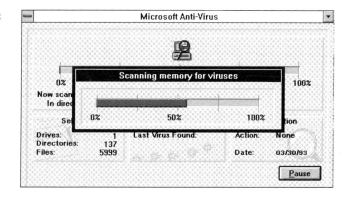

Figure 5. After checking memory for viruses, Anti-Virus now checks every file on the selected disks for known viruses. This can take a few minutes, depending on the size of your disk.

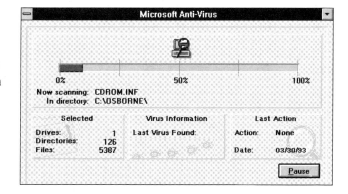

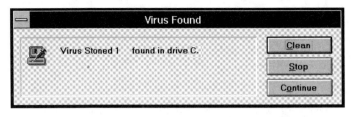

Figure 6. If Anti-Virus detects a virus, it alerts you and asks whether you want to *Clean* this virus from the system. (If you had selected *Detect and Clean* initially, Anti-Virus would automatically remove this virus.)

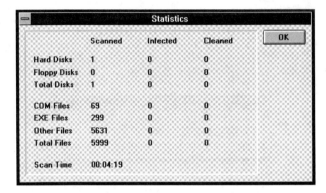

Figure 7. After Anti-Virus has scanned the selected disks and cleaned any viruses from the system, the program displays a series of statistics about the process.

SETTING ANTI-VIRUS OPTIONS

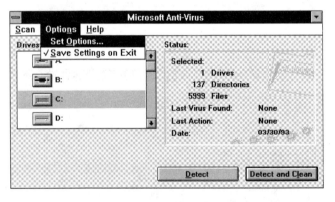

Figure 8. If you select *Set Options* from the Options menu, you can set exactly how much protection from viruses you would like Anti-Virus to provide.

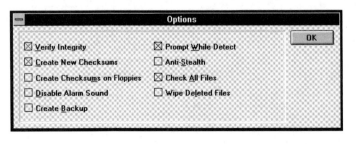

Figure 9. If you select the *Verify Integrity* check box, Anti-Virus checks for infected executable files and alerts you when it finds infected files.

If you select the *Create New Checksums* option, Anti-Virus can tell whether executable files have changed between scans by creating a list of file information in each directory it scans. As viruses generally change the size of executable files, this is a good way to determine whether an unknown virus has infected your system.

The *Create Checksums on Floppies* does the same thing as *Create New Checksums*, but on floppy disks.

Disable Alarm Sound, when selected, tells Anti-Virus that it shouldn't play a sound when it finds a virus.

Create Backup is an option that you should use with caution. When you select this option, Anti-Virus creates a backup of any infected file before it cleans it. This means that the virus is not totally removed from your system. It may, however, be your only alternative, if removing the virus means removing the program file itself.

Prompt While Detect determines whether Anti-Virus prompts you when it discovers viruses and infected files during a *Detect*.

Anti-Stealth protection is designed for viruses that can alter executable programs without appearing to have changed them at all, thus avoiding checksum tests. When you check this option (make sure you also select the *Verify Integrity* option), Anti-Virus performs a more detailed examination of executable files.

The *Check All Files* option means that Anti-Virus checks all files during a scan, not just executable, program, or program overlay files.

The *Wipe Deleted Files* option forces Anti-Virus to ensure that you cannot undelete any deleted program file (one that was infected with a virus).

BACKUP

Backup is a program designed to let you quickly and easily back up data to another disk or floppy disks. Backup is particularly useful because it can compress files as it backs them up, and also allow large files or several disks to be used during the backup.

You start *Backup* by double-clicking on the *Backup* icon in the *Microsoft Tools* program group.

USING BACKUP FOR THE FIRST TIME

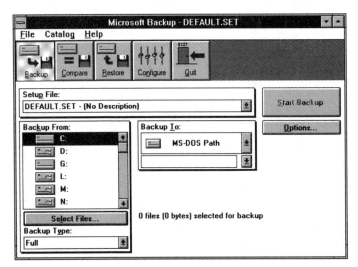

Figure 10. This figure displays the Backup opening screen. The very first time you use Backup, it takes you through a series of steps designed to let Backup determine what hardware you have and what procedures you want it to use to back up files.

You need one or two blank floppy disks, as it performs a test backup of your MS-DOS files. Until it completes this test, follow the instructions given on screen.

The buttons across the top of the Backup window let you select the function you want:

Backup—back up files from the hard disk to other media such as floppy disks.

Compare—check the integrity of your backup. This option ensures that errors have not been made during backup.

Restore—copy files from the backup back onto the hard disk.

Configure—set backup options.

BACKING UP DATA

Figure 11. Before you back up data, make sure that you have selected the *Backup* button.

Figure 12. First, select the data that you want to back up. From the *Backup From* disk list, select the disk with the data. Here, we have selected drive C:.

If you select a drive by double-clicking on it, Backup assumes you want to back up the entire disk by displaying "All Files" alongside the drive name. If you double-click again this removes this display.

The *Select Files* button allows you to select exactly which files from the selected drive you would like to back up.

Backup From:

	C:
	D:
	G:
	L:
	M:
	N:

Select Files...

Backup Type:

Full

Figure 13. Clicking on the *Select Files* button displays a list of files, much like you see in the Windows File Manager. From here, you select the files that you want to back up.

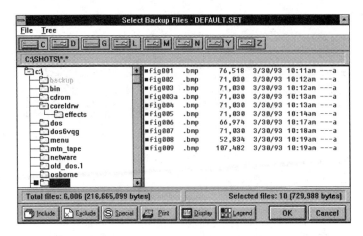

Figure 14. You select files by clicking on the directory (on the left-hand side) or on files in a directory (on the right-hand side), and pressing the Spacebar. Selected files appear in red.

You can deselect files and directories by pressing the Spacebar once again.

Once you have selected the files you wish to backup, you click on the *OK* button.

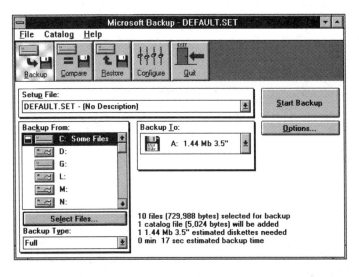

Figure 15. When you return to the startup screen, Backup lists statistics about the files you selected, and gives you an estimate of the number of floppy disks you need and the amount of time that it will take.

You can, if you wish, change the *Backup Type* from the drop-down list at the bottom of the screen.

A *Full* backup backs up all selected files.

An *Incremental* backup backs up all files that have changed since the last *Full* backup and sets the Archive attribute of these flags to indicate that you have backed them up.

A *Differential* backup performs a similar function, but does not reset the archive flag of the files you have backed up.

Figure 16. Finally, you must decide where to back up the selected data. You would normally choose a floppy disk drive, but you could choose another hard disk, or even a directory on the current hard disk. In this example, we have selected drive A.

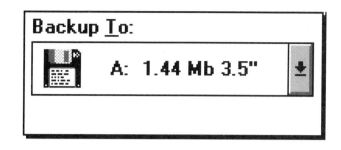

Once you have made these selections, click on the *Start Backup* button to start the backup.

Figure 17. Backup keeps you fully informed as it backs up data and asks you to insert new disks if necessary.

It is very important that you label the floppy disks that you have used during the backup as Disk #1, Disk #2, etc., otherwise you will have trouble when you try to restore files.

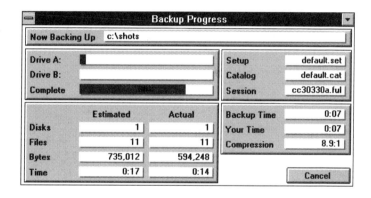

Figure 18. When it is finished, Backup lets you know with this alert and tells you how many files it has backed up.

It is important to keep the disks in a safe place once you have backed up your data.

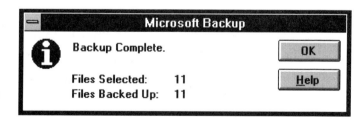

COMPARING FILES

To ensure that the data you have backed up has not been corrupted, you may want to compare the backed up files to the original on disk to ensure they are the same.

Review the section in this chapter on **Backup Options** to see how you can make Backup perform a *Compare* operation automatically as it backs up data.

Figure 19. Select the *Compare* button to compare your backed up and original files.

Compare is similar to *Backup* in that you select the disk to compare from and the files you want to compare with.

Backup then asks you to insert floppy disks from the backup set and compares the data. If it finds any differences, you should select the *Configure* button and do a compatibility test.

RESTORING DATA

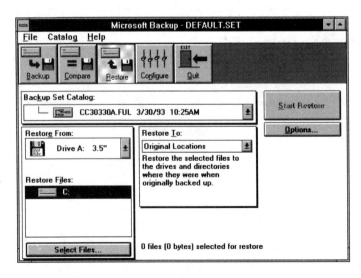

Figure 20. At some stage you may need to restore data from the backup set back onto your system. To do this, select the *Restore* button and Backup starts the operation by asking you how you want the files restored.

Figure 21. The most fail-safe way of restoring data is the *Retrieve* command in the **Catalog** menu, which retrieves catalog information from the backup data.

This catalog information lets Backup know exactly what directories and files it backed up.

Figure 22. Select the drive on which you backed up the data. When you click on *OK* in the *Retrieve Catalog* dialog box, Backup asks you to insert the last disk from the backup set you want to restore. This is where Backup stores catalog information.

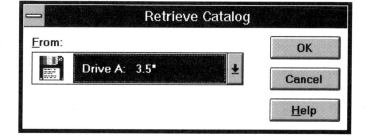

It then loads the catalog information automatically. (If you receive a warning that the catalog file already exists on the hard disk, don't worry, just select *OK* to overwrite it.)

Once Backup loads the catalog file, it displays the Backup window of Figure 20. From here, you can choose the *Select Files* button, or double-click on the drive icon in the *Restore Files* list to restore all files.

Once you have selected which files you want, select the *Start Restore* button to restore the files.

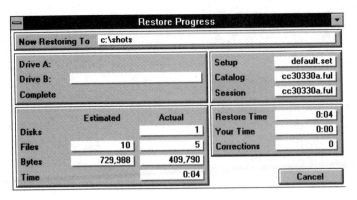

Figure 23. Backup shows you various statistics as it restores the files; it also prompts you to insert disks if there is more than one in the set.

BACKUP OPTIONS

When you select the *Backup* button from the Backup startup screen (Figure 10), you can select the *Options* button to set your backup preferences.

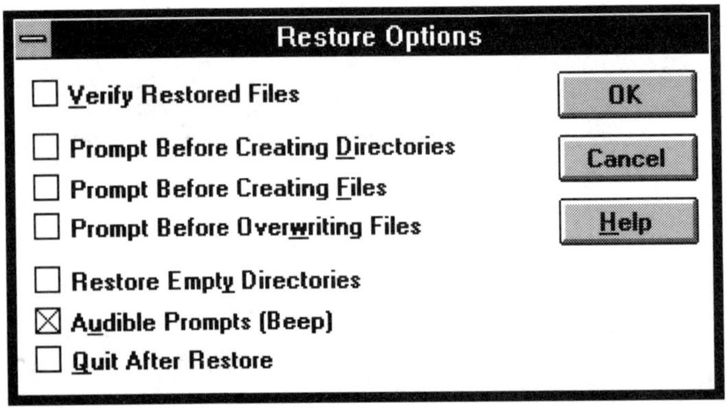

Figure 24. The *Restore Options* dialog box lets you select how Backup operates when restoring.

If you select the *Verify Restored Files* option, Backup compares each file as it backs up. This slows the backup process down considerably but ensures that the backup information is secure.

The *Prompt Before...* options, if you select them, force Backup to check with you as it creates new files or directories, or it overwrites files during a restore.

The *Restore Empty Directories* option makes sure that Backup recreates all directories during a restore, even those that do not have any files.

UNDELETING FILES

Microsoft Undelete is a program that allows you to rescue files that you might have accidentally deleted.

You start *Undelete* by double-clicking on the *Undelete* icon in the *Microsoft Tools* program group.

Figure 25. Using Undelete is quite simple—all you really have to do is select the directory or drive that contains the files that you have deleted.

You can select drives and directories and search for files using the appropriate buttons from the top of the Undelete screen.

In this example, Undelete cannot find any deleted files in the *C:\win31* directory.

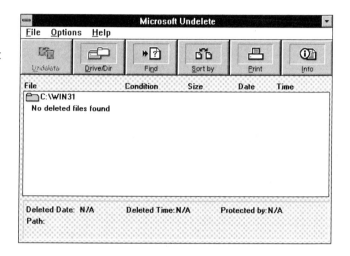

Figure 26. Here we selected a new directory, using the *Drive/Dir* button. Undelete lists all deleted files it found, along with all of the file details.

The most important file detail is the *Condition*—this gives you an idea how likely it is that you can undelete a particular file. In this case, only one file, *?ig024.bmp*, is given any chance at all—most files are marked with the *Condition* "Destroyed."

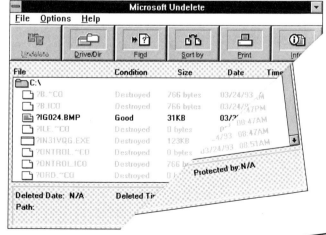

To undelete a file, select the file you are after and click on the *Undelete* button.

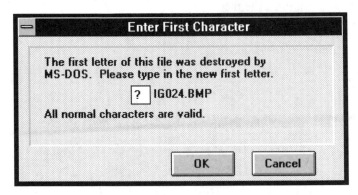

Figure 27. When you delete a file, MS-DOS destroys the first letter of that filename. Therefore, to undelete the file, it must have the first letter. Undelete prompts you for that letter.

Enter a letter (it does not really matter what the letter is, as long as the filename makes sense), and click on *OK.*

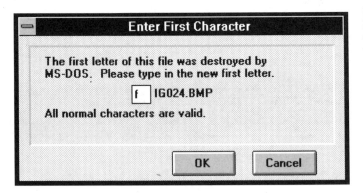

Figure 28. Here we have added the letter "f." Undelete tells us that all the normal characters are valid, so the file is OK.

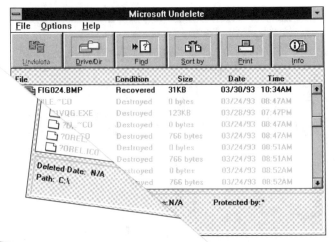

Figure 29. If Undelete is successful with the file, the file appears in the *Undelete* window, as *fig024.bmp* appears here.

WARNING: If you delete a file accidentally, do not copy to or create any files on the disk from which the file was deleted before attempting to unerase it. The more data that you write to a disk, the less chance you have of recovering a deleted file.

Index

printing, 91
renaming, 92
safeguarding, 92
selecting, 85-87
selecting across directories, 88
viewing, 90
naming conventions, 22
printing, 61
renaming, 47-48
repairing, 67
restoring, 128
types, 23-24
undeleting, 57
Files command, 159
Find command, MS-DOS Editor, 115
finding files, 90
finding text, MS-DOS Editor, 115
floppy disks, 16
For command, 155
Format command
Microsoft DoubleSpace, 139
using, 62
formatting disks, 19, 62
fragmentation. *See* Microsoft Defrag
full backup, 125
full pathname, 49

G

Goto command, 155
graphics adapter. *See* video adapter
graphics mode, MS-DOS Shell, 77

H

hard disk, 18
hardware, 2

help
MS-DOS Editor, 106
MS-DOS Shell, 76
Help Path command, MS-DOS Editor, 118
Hercules Graphics Card (HGC), 13
Hidden file attribute
purpose, 58, 93
setting, 59
setting, MS-DOS Shell, 93
high-density disks, 17
High Memory Area (HMA), 10, 161
Himem.sys device driver, 160-162
HMA. *See* High Memory Area

I

icons, MS-DOS Shell, 70-71, 94
If command, 155
impact printer, 13
incremental backup, 125
input, 6
input and output devices, 6, 11
Insert mode, 107, 148

J

jump
to label in batch file, 155

K

keyboards, 6
kilobytes, 9

More from Peachpit Press. . .

Desktop Publishing Secrets
Robert Eckhardt, Bob Weibel, and Ted Nace
Hundreds of the best desktop publishing tips from 5 years of *Publish* magazine. *(550 pages)*

Letter to a Computer Novice
Larry Magid
An introduction to personal computers that assumes no prior technical knowledge. *(200 pages, available Summer 1993)*

The Little DOS 6 Book
Kay Yarborough Nelson
A quick and accessible guide to DOS 6. Includes numerous tips, tricks, and charts of keyboard shortcuts. *(160 pages)*

The Little Laptop Book
Steve Cummings
Provides information on using applications and utilities, printing on the road, and telecommunication. *(192 pages)*

The Little OS/2 Book, 2.1 Edition
Kay Yarborough Nelson
Loaded with useful information, this is an introduction to IBM's powerful operating system. *(176 pages)*

The Little WordPerfect Book
Skye Lininger
Gives step-by-step instructions for setting page margins, typing text, navigating with the cursor keys, and more. *(160 pages)*

The Little WordPerfect for Windows Book
Kay Yarborough Nelson
A quick and accessible guide that includes numerous tips and charts of keyboard shortcuts. *(200 pages)*

Mastering Corel Draw 3
Chris Dickman
Provides beginning lessons and advanced tips on using this remarkable drawing program for Windows. Includes two disks. *(600 pages)*

PageMaker 4: An Easy Desk Reference
Robin Williams
A totally thorough, indispensable reference book for PageMaker 4.0. *(768 page)*

PageMaker 5: Visual QuickStart Guide
Webster and Associates
Provides a highly visual introduction to desktop publishing in PageMaker 5.0 for the PC. *(176 pages, available Summer 1993)*

The PC is not a typewriter
Robin Williams
Explains the principles behind the techniques for professional typesetting and how they can be utilized on the desktop. *(96 pages)*

The QuarkXPress Book, Windows Edition
David Blatner and Bob Weibel
Peachpit's best-selling, highly acclaimed Quark book is now available for Windows users. *(576 pages)*

Ventura Tips and Tricks, 3rd Edition
Ted Nace and Daniel Will-Harris
Performance tips, advice on using Ventura utilities, useful tables and charts, and clear explanations. *(790 pages)*

The Windows 3.1 Bible
Fred Davis
Everything you ever wanted to know about Windows 3.1, compiled by one of America's leading Windows experts. *(1,152 pages)*

The Windows 3.1 Font Book
David Angell and Brent Heslop
How to manage, choose, and use fonts. Covers both TrueType and PostScript, and offers a comprehensive listing of font vendors. *(184 pages)*

Word for Windows Essentials
Geoffrey Mandel
A well-indexed, well-organized book to get beginners familiar with Word's powerful tools. *(216 pages)*

WordPerfect: Desktop Publishing in Style, 2nd Edition
Daniel Will-Harris
Peachpit's popular guide to producing documents with WordPerfect 5.1 or 5.0. *(650 pages)*

Order Form

to order, call:
(800) 283-9444 or (510) 548-4393 or (510) 548-5991 (fax)

#	Title	Price	Total
	Desktop Publishing Secrets	27.95	
	DOS 6: Visual QuickStart Guide	12.00	
	Letter to a Computer Novice *(Summer 1993)*	16.00	
	The Little DOS 6 Book	13.00	
	The Little Laptop Book	14.95	
	The Little OS/2 Book, 2.1 Edition	13.00	
	The Little WordPerfect Book	12.95	
	The Little WordPerfect for Windows Book	12.95	
	Mastering Corel Draw 3 (with 2 disks)	38.00	
	PageMaker 4: An Easy Desk Reference	29.95	
	PageMaker 5: Visual QuickStart Guide *(Summer 1993)*	13.00	
	The PC is not a typewriter	9.95	
	The QuarkXPress Book, Windows Edition	28.00	
	Ventura Tips and Tricks, 3rd Edition	27.95	
	Windows 3.1 Bible	28.00	
	Windows 3.1 Font Book	12.95	
	Word for Windows Essentials	14.00	
	WordPerfect: Desktop Publishing in Style, 2nd Edition	23.95	

SHIPPING:	First Item	Each Additional	Subtotal	
UPS Ground	$4	$1	8.25% Tax (CA only)	
UPS Blue	$7	$2		
Canada	$6	$4	Shipping	
Overseas	$14	$14	**TOTAL**	

Name			
Company			
Address			
City	State		Zip
Phone	Fax		
❏ Check enclosed	❏ Visa		❏ MasterCard
Company purchase order #			
Credit card #	Expiration Date		

Peachpit Press, Inc. • 2414 Sixth Street • Berkeley, CA • 94710
Your satisfaction is guaranteed or your money will be cheerfully refunded!